The
MIND, BODY & SPIRIT
COMPANION

The

MIND, BODY & SPIRIT COMPANION

Exercises and meditations to free
your spirit and fulfil your dreams

DUNCAN BAIRD PUBLISHERS

LONDON

The Mind, Body & Spirit Companion

Published in 2006 by Duncan Baird Publishers
Sixth Floor, Castle House, 75–76 Wells Street, London, W1T 3QH

Copyright © Bookspan 2006
Text copyright © Duncan Baird Publishers 2006
Artwork copyright © Duncan Baird Publishers 2006
Created and designed by Bookspan and Duncan Baird Publishers

Managing Designer: Daniel Sturges
Designer: Rebecca Johns
Editors: Ingrid Court-Jones and Rebecca Miles
Illustrations commissioned by Gail Jones
For illustration credits, see p.240

British Library Cataloguing-in-Publication Data:
A CIP record for this book is available from the British Library

ISBN-10: 1-84483-306-2
ISBN-13: 9-781844-833061

1 3 5 7 9 10 8 6 4 2
Typeset in Bell MT
Colour reproduction by Colourscan, Singapore
Printed by Imago, Thailand

"A single gentle rain makes the grass many shades greener. So our prospects brighten on the influx of brighter thoughts."

Henry David Thoreau (1817–1862)

Contents

CHAPTER 4:
INSPIRING THE FUTURE 172

CHAPTER 5:
INSPIRING THE SPIRIT 202

INTRODUCTION

We all have within ourselves the capacity to create a life of self-awareness, empathy, and love; to be creative in all our projects and relationships; to find contentment in ourselves, in each other, and in the world around us; and to bring joy and fulfillment to loved ones, family, friends, and colleagues. These are some of the destinations to which a journey of positive change and inner growth can satisfyingly lead. *Live Well with One Spirit* provides a set of helpful signposts along the way.

The book is organized around the theme of inspirations —for Mind, Karma, Body, Future, and Spirit—with suggested practices, affirmations, goals, projects, and insights to establish a firm foundation of well-being. The text offers wise, practical advice and thought-provoking ideas to encourage personal and spiritual development and healthy, rewarding relationships. Included are dozens of exercises, spanning dreams, creativity, healing, massage, animals, harmony, self-awareness, and more to fulfill and strengthen our inner being. Positive affirmations, as well as quotations to inform and inspire, range from the Zen and Taoist classics to modern men and women of wisdom, such as Nelson Mandela and Mother Teresa.

Since 2001, One Spirit has published an annual *Book of Days*—an illustrated daybook which now has a tremendous following across America. *Live Well with One Spirit* features, for the first time, the best illustrations and weekly exercises from our six-year archive of these daybooks. Powerful, transcendent, and rich, *Live Well* proves a wise companion for all who seek to live healthily and happily in self-awareness.

CHAPTER 1

INSPIRING THE MIND

From time to time we all feel the need to take a break from the seemingly ceaseless mental chatter that accompanies busy modern lives. Putting aside even five or ten minutes a day to quieten our minds has a hugely beneficial effect on our general well-being. Spend time with the texts, exercises, quotations, and affirmations in the following pages, and incorporate into your daily life those ideas that speak to you most deeply. Give your mind some space and time to relax and expand into new ideas—this is a precious gift to yourself.

"To the mind that is still, the whole universe surrenders."
Lao Tzu (c.604–c.531 BC)

MEDITATION

Awaken from the Daydream

Zen master Chuang Tzu dreamed he was a butterfly. When he awoke he didn't know if he was himself dreaming he was a butterfly or a butterfly dreaming he was himself. Certainly, consciousness can become dream-like, a mist around reality. In meditation the aim is to set yourself free from the daydream of consciousness. Let go of all thoughts and emotions. Stop striving to understand. Just be, and true understanding will dawn.

"Learn to wish that everything should come to pass exactly as it does."
Epictetus (c.55–c.135 AD)

Sea of Calm

Prepare for meditation by counting backward from fifty. Visualize yourself rowing a boat toward a peaceful island. With each pull of the oars you count, feel your movements become more languid, your breathing slow down, and your strokes become longer and more relaxed. When you reach zero, see yourself arriving on your island to begin your meditation.

A Candle Meditation

Whichever posture you adopt in your meditation—full lotus, half-lotus, or sitting on a chair—be sure to keep your back straight and your head upright. Close your eyes, empty your mind of thoughts, and imagine the flame of a candle. See its flickering. Visualize it as your innate spiritual awareness.

Your Inner Flame

A good object to use for meditation is an *actual* candle flame. Gaze at the flame, observing its shifting colors. Imagine the flame entering your being. Then look at it for another minute ot two. Close your eyes, aware of the afterglow behind your eyelids, and for several minutes hold the image in your mind. As you meditate on the flame, lose all sense of its separateness.

"With time and patience the mulberry leaf becomes a silk gown."
Chinese proverb

A FLOWER MEDITATION

Meditate on the chrysanthemum flower, an Eastern
symbol of good fortune. Either use a real flower, or the
stylized illustration above. Observe the flower (real or
depicted), scanning its main features. Do not look for
meaning in it; just allow its shapes, lines, and colors to
penetrate your consciousness. Be aware that the image is
both in front of you and inside your mind.

Meditate on Clouds

Clouds make a useful focus for a simple but effective meditation. Sit somewhere comfortable inside your home, close your eyes, and, as random thoughts enter your mind, attach each one to an imaginary cloud, letting it float lazily across the blue sky of your consciousness until it is out of sight. Finish the exercise after about five minutes—feeling relaxed and refreshed.

*"Wherever you go, you will always bear yourself about with you,
and so you will always find yourself."*
Thomas à Kempis (c.1380–1471)

Meditate on a Mandala

A mandala is a deeply spiritual symbol, used in meditation. The best-known examples are those from Tibet, which depict the palace of the gods in various ways. By entering the spirit of a mandala, we can attain a sense of oneness with the cosmos. Above is a simplified mandala that is typical in combining the symbolism of the circle (eternity) with that of the square (the created world). In the center is a lotus flower. Sit comfortably and focus on the image without worrying about its precise religious significance. Enter it like someone entering a room. Take in all the features but do not engage with them intellectually. Let the symbolism seep into your unconscious mind.

Mantra Meditation

Another tried-and-tested method to focus the mind in meditation is to recite a mantra—a word or phrase that is repeated over and over. A mantra can be any spiritual insight that empowers and calms us, such as *I am spirit* or *I am peace*. Or it can be one of the more traditional incantations, such as *Om*—pronounced in three syllables, "a—u—m." Simply repeat your chosen syllable, word, or phrase to yourself, and let the sounds fill your consciousness. By reciting the "root" mantra, *Om*, we energize and center the body, and partake of the power of creation.

An Empty Vessel

This Buddhist meditation heightens awareness of your physical space. Visualize the form of an empty teacup, and the space into which the tea is poured. Would the cup be a cup without its outer form and inner space? Could the cup exist without the emptiness around it? Reflect on the subtle interplay between form and emptiness in everything around you.

PLANETARY PERCEPTION

To stretch your mental horizons, it helps to visualize different aspects of the heavens. For example, all planets experience day and night, as they rotate on their axes. Use the planets as the subject of a three-dimensional meditation. Make your mind more supple by visualizing the complexities of the solar system.

AFFIRMATION

Beyond my grasp lies a universe of infinite wonder and complexity—this is my spirit's home.

M I N D F U L N E S S

✦

The Fruits of Awareness

Practice mindfulness next time you go for a stroll in the park or a walk in the country. Rather than using nature as a backdrop to your thoughts, put preoccupations on hold, and give your undivided attention to each living thing you see. As you do so, a sense of deep connection will gradually ripen at the core of your being.

"We can do no great things—only small things with great love."
Mother Teresa of Calcutta (1910–1997)

The Value of Repetition

Performed in the right frame of mind, simple, repetitive tasks such as washing windows and serving food can help us open up to the spirit—our left brains quieten and our right brains become more receptive. And there is an inherent dignity and purpose in such work. As a Zen master said, "Before enlightenment, chop wood and carry water; after enlightenment, chop wood and carry water."

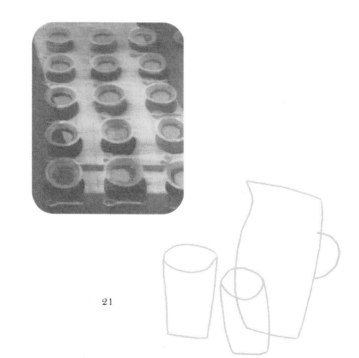

21

Hitting the Target

Zen master Chuang Tzu asserted that the need to win can drain an archer of his power. By focusing on what we are doing, we can be both mindful and spontaneous. This frees us from any thought of winning and losing, and allows us to fully experience the moment. Try to draw your bow (metaphorically speaking, of course) without being attached to concern about the outcome. Whether or not you hit the target will be determined by how successful you are in freeing yourself from the burden of anxiety.

Complete Presence

Practice mindfulness by spending ten minutes consciously trying to be fully aware of the rich and complex sensory experience of each moment—appreciate the shapes and colors of everything you see, the sounds and smells around you, and the touch of air and fabric against your skin. If your mind tries to resist such discipline by sliding out of the present moment into the past or future, simply bring your attention back to the present moment.

S E L F - B E L I E F

BE FAIR TO YOURSELF

Before we can truly give our love to others we must first learn to love and respect ourselves, but often we are our own harshest critics. Each evening spend a few minutes looking back over your day to give yourself the opportunity to learn from your errors. Forgive yourself for them, note and praise your successes, and reaffirm your friendship with yourself before going to bed.

"Those of us who know the truth are not equal to those of us who love the truth."
Confucius (551–479 BC)

The Treasure Chest

Reflect on the treasures within you—gifts such as love, strength, courage, and empathy. Make a point of focusing on these positive qualities; learn to trust and respect all you have and all you are. If you are able to do that in your everyday life, your inner treasure chest will spring open and your gifts will be revealed to all around you.

"In order to find Perfect Wisdom, one must go through the door of one's self-nature."
Chinese proverb (7th century AD)

Connect with the Cosmos

Our lives can sometimes seem insignificant, but we can transform this feeling by remembering our place in the cosmos. Pick out a constellation in the night sky—for example, your star sign if you can find it—and know that your life, like each of the millions of stars in the heavens, adds light and beauty to the universe. In the midst of all this vastness, there is a place for you, and your life interconnects with the whole.

The Maze and the Unicorn

Imagine the hero Theseus enters the labyrinth to fight the monstrous Minotaur—but instead of the Minotaur he finds the rare, shy unicorn. Often the difficulties or dangers we expect never materialize—and instead we have a good experience, not a bad one. Never prejudge events. Good things can happen on the days we most dread.

A Voyage to the Center of the Self

Visualize yourself floating in the warm ocean. On the sea bed you spot the wreck of a galleon. You swim down and enter the ship. The farther in you go, the brighter the water becomes. At the center lies a chest of precious objects: each one is an aspect of your true self. Swim back to the surface, relaxed in the knowledge of your worth.

AFFIRMATION
I have a wealth of knowledge and intuition to tap.
Time spent in quiet contemplation allows these
inner riches to emerge.

PROJECT YOUR INNER SELF

See yourself as significant—not just a cog in the machine. You are the leading actor of your own drama, in charge of your own destiny. There are some aspects of life you cannot alter, such as the personalities or motivations of other people, but you can make big changes if you choose to. Act in the full knowledge of your powers, which are both a gift and a responsibility.

"All the knowledge I possess everyone else can acquire, but my heart is all my own."
Johann Wolfgang von Goethe (1749–1832)

Virtue's Reward

Prizes and trophies are merely symbols of our attainments and as such they often have no practical value. Think of your own most significant successes in symbolic terms: your virtues may not have brought you material reward, but their effects on others, however modest, are meaningful emblems of your achievement.

"Don't judge each day by the harvest you reap but by the seeds that you plant."
Robert Louis Stevenson (1850–1894)

STILLNESS

The Eye of the Storm

In the eye of the storm there is stillness. No matter what happens at any moment during any day, however hectic or troublesome things appear, and however many tasks we seem to be trying to do at once, we need only to turn inward to find a haven of peace. To access your haven, close your eyes and imagine a still and gentle light within you. Focus on the tranquility it brings.

"Keep the peace within yourself, then you can also bring peace to others."
Thomas à Kempis (1380–1471)

The Beehive

Worries often buzz around in our heads like bees around a hive, creating a perpetual background hum of anxiety. To help retune your mind, imagine a hive surrounded by honeybees, with each bee representing a niggling problem. Now visualize the bees disappearing one at a time into the hive, and notice how the buzz in your mind quiets down.

Stress Ballooning

Another way to banish worries is to imagine you are loading them into the basket of a hot-air balloon. In your mind's eye, release the balloon from its moorings and see it rise into the sky. Your problems become more and more remote as the balloon gets smaller and smaller. Watch it drift over the horizon, taking all your worries with it.

"How refreshing to hear the whinny of a packhorse when a burden is lifted off its back!"
Zen saying

GALLOPING EMOTIONS

Sometimes our emotions behave like horses, straining to break free of our control. When this happens, try to step back for a moment and remain calm. Bear in mind that your horses can be controlled—they respond to will, intelligence, and reason. If you mentally tell them to stay in their stalls, they will do so. It is only with your permission that they can break free.

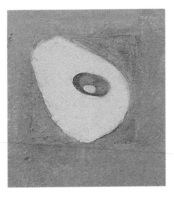

Emotional Release

A natural response to anger is to clench your fist. Paradoxically, you can use this reflex to relax. Pick a small, hard object, such as a stone, and place it in the palm of your hand. Squeeze the object as hard as you can, then release it. Rock the object gently in your hand as if making peace with it. Do this every time you feel a surge of emotion, and let the feelings pass away.

Nature's Balm

Sit outside in a peaceful garden or park and let the soothing sounds of nature help you relax your body and still your mind. Close your eyes and tune in to the birds' singing, the leaves rustling in the breeze, or water splashing in a fountain. "Extend" your listening as far as you can. Try to stay focused in this way for five minutes.

"Do not anticipate trouble, or worry about what may never happen.
Keep in the sunlight."
Benjamin Franklin (1706–1790)

S E L F - A W A R E N E S S

◆

Self to Self

The relationship at the heart of our lives is the one we have with ourselves. No other relationship can be an adequate substitute. Regularly spending short periods of time alone will help you cultivate this key aspect of your life.

Your Tree of Life

By meditating on your "tree of life," you will develop a stronger sense of self. Begin by tracing your way back to your roots—to the infuence of home, society, family, and friends. Notice the marks on the tree trunk, the scars that you have acquired while finding your place in the world. Appreciate the fruits of the tree—the achievements you are proud of. Nurture its buds, for these are your goals and dreams, which will one day shape your future.

AFFIRMATION
Peace begins at home. When I come from a place of
inner peace, I see peace all around me.

A MOOD DIARY

Personality is a solid core with fluid edges—the edges are our changing moods. To improve our understanding of ourselves, it helps to keep a journal of our moods' fluctuations. By analyzing our written observations and looking for patterns in them, we can pinpoint the best and worst times to undertake important activities. Also, we may be able to anticipate what's coming when, and hence make adjustments or allowances accordingly.

Self-Counseling

Learn to be your own wise counselor. Close your eyes and picture your alter ego sitting opposite you in a chair. What questions does your other self ask you? What are the most honest answers to those questions? Do you trust the counsel of your alter ego? If so, open your eyes and set about heeding your own advice—it is the best you will ever hear!

"Through what is near, one understands what is far away."
Hsun Tzu (300–c.230 BC)

Many Faces

We create many identities for ourselves—the roles we play for others in life's various situations. Trouble arises when these roles obscure our understanding of who we really are. We might say "I'm a nurse," or "I'm an extrovert", or "I'm a coward." Self-realization comes from throwing away these labels and focusing on the true, inner person. Each day spend five minutes freeing yourself from one of your labels—and see how much lighter you feel.

The Mirror

This exercise helps you distinguish how you see yourself from how others see you. Take twenty minutes to write a list of all your positive qualities, and draw an image of this positive you. Next day, write a list of all the qualities that other people might see in you, and draw an image of this person. If there are differences, ask yourself if, to narrow the gap, you need to change the way you behave or present yourself to the world.

Life's Jigsaw Puzzle

We have so many roles defined by our relationships with others that we can lose track of our true selves. If this describes you, think of yourself as a jigsaw puzzle. It may be difficult to see the whole because some pieces don't seem to fit together. But, with work, you will find the place for each piece and the true picture will emerge.

"Truth emerges more readily from error than from confusion."
Francis Bacon (1561–1626)

D R E A M S

◆

The Language of the Unconscious

By offering us the chance to eavesdrop on the nightly conversation between our unconscious and conscious minds, dreams can help us understand ourselves better. Typically, they use symbols to represent an idea or feeling that cannot easily be put into words. Sometimes a symbol might be personal to the dreamer, at other times it might draw upon traditional associations—for example, flowers to suggest a personal blossoming, or water to represent life itself.

The Art of Interpretation

When trying to understand a dream, it's easy to rush into an obvious interpretation without allowing time for alternative meanings to suggest themselves. To counteract this, spend time contemplating the dream and the symbols it contained. Consider the dream scenario from the perspectives of each of the characters in the dream, until a multitude of meanings emerge.

PROBLEM SOLVING

When you dream, your mind is released from the inhibitions of your waking life, allowing the hidden power of intuition free rein to operate. Before sleep, think about a problem that you have been unable to solve logically—your unconscious may provide an ingenious solution which your rational mind could never have reached.

AFFIRMATION
I rest in tranquility and divine grace. Even as I sleep, I am happy, healthy, and fulfilled.

Dream Haven

Some people are able to cue restful dreams by meditating on an image that they associate with happiness or peace—perhaps their home, a soothing landscape, or a cherished friend—for a few minutes before bedtime. As they meditate on the image, it penetrates their unconscious, where it can exert benevolent influence all through the night to help ward off troubled dreams.

"A dream which is not interpreted is like a letter which is not read."
The Talmud

Dream Journal

As soon as we begin really *wanting* to remember our dreams, we are well on the way to success. Upon waking, try to recall the night's dreams in as much detail as possible and jot them down in a special dream journal you keep by your bedside. Don't delay writing them until later, as even the most vivid dreams can quickly fade or become distorted. Note how you felt as well as what you saw.

DECISIONS & CHANGE

✦

Step by Step

Be proactive in decision-making. Make unimportant decisions quickly, to give yourself more time for the important ones. When facing big decisions, don't be daunted—just work toward the answer logically, step by step.

Follow the Tao

Taoism is an Eastern philosophy based on the principle that life involves ceaseless movement within a grand cosmic harmony. Problems arise when we attempt to resist or control the natural pattern of change. You can restore harmony in your life by following the Tao—that is, by "going with the flow," accepting the ever-changing pattern of life without either judgment or resistance.

"We shall steer safely through every storm, so long as our own heart is right, our intention forever fervent, our courage steadfast and our trust fixed in God."
St. Francis de Sales (1567–1622)

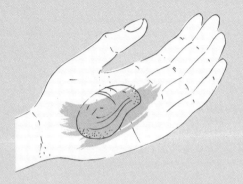

A PEBBLE TALISMAN

Carry a pebble with you (maybe a varnished one) to use as a kind of talisman—a focus for your most cherished intentions. These might include staying calm under stress, or asserting your point of view in a difficult environment, or abandoning an undesirable habit of some kind. Hold your pebble in your hand, and swear on it your promises to yourself. Then keep it in your pocket as a continual reminder of your resolutions. Hold your pebble in a spirit of resolve and affirmation whenever the occasion arises.

A Sense of Balance

Many of us struggle to balance our lives. It's not uncommon to find ourselves devoting too much time and effort to issues that are important to others, but not to us. To redress this imbalance, take time to reassess what really matters to you. Then, set yourself goals, and change your priorities to help you reach those goals.

"Today, well lived, makes every yesterday a dream of happiness and every tomorrow a vision of hope. Look well, therefore, to this day."
Sanskrit proverb

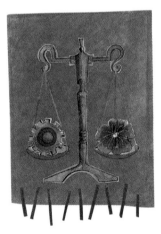

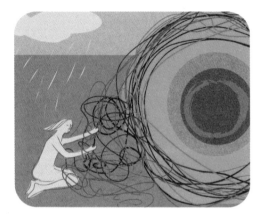

Unravel Your Problems

When struggling to find a solution to a complicated problem, try to identify different strands within it and work on these one at a time. Avoid letting the various individual difficulties compound into a single, giant predicament—the tendency sometimes known as "catastrophizing." Be satisfied to achieve a partial solution as a starting-point for further improvement. Complex tangles take time to form and time to unravel.

Breaking Free

Habits can be practical aids in our lives, but often we retain behavioral patterns that are no longer appropriate. We do this because they give us the comfort of familiarity. Breaking the bonds of habit may seem a daunting or formidable prospect, but why not try it? Freedom tastes sweeter than comfort.

Spider Power

When you find yourself working in vain to solve a problem or to make an important change in your life, always ask yourself whether it would be helpful to enlist help from others—even if all they do for you is listen. Some problems cease to be daunting when tackled collectively. As the Ethiopian proverb puts it, "When spiders unite, they can tie up a lion."

AFFIRMATION

I will change when I wish or need to change, when the moment for change is ripe. Until then I will remain as I am.

SHINING STAR

Your best actions not only make a positive contribution to your life by shaping the circumstances around you: they also act as a beacon to others, who may be inspired to follow your lead. When attempting an especially difficult course of action, gain strength from the thought that you will be serving others by setting them a good example.

"First say to yourself what you would be; and then do what you have to do."
Epictetus (c.55–c.135 AD)

49

A C C E P T A N C E

✦

Trust in Life's Flow

Many people bring a great deal of unnecessary anxiety upon themselves by earnestly wishing—or willing—that things were otherwise. When chance seems to be working against you, you will waste precious strength if you struggle to turn back the tide. Try letting go and trusting in the natural flow of events. Whatever is yours will come to you in due course.

Everything in Its Season

Like the years with their changing seasons, our lives have a natural pattern. If you find that life is not unfolding according to your personal vision, it may be merely that the time is not yet right for the particular development you have in mind. Meditate on these ancient Egyptian symbols of the seasons. Trust in the natural flow of events and revelations. Have faith that everything that is meant to happen will happen, at just the right time.

"Could it be that my whisper was already born before my lips?"
Osip Mandelshtam (1891–1938)

One Thing at a Time

When you feel overwhelmed and stressed, it is easy to rush and try to do too many things at once. Whether at home or at work, choose one job and focus on it fully. If chores clamor for your attention, quiet your mind for a few minutes, then make this affirmation: "In thinking of only one thing at once, I am accepting an important truth: all other things can wait."

Riding the Storm

We all have periods when we feel overwhelmed by circumstance—unable to keep our life balanced. It helps to visualize such times as stormclouds—part of life's ever-changing weather system. If we learn to hunker down and wait for the clouds to pass, we may see that even at the heart of the storm our essential self is invulnerable.

"We could never learn to be brave and patient, if there were only joy in the world."
Helen Keller (1880–1968)

A GENTLE ENCOUNTER

Imagine you are in a boat on a river and another boat collides with yours. Although you may initially be angry, how would that serve you? Make an effort always to conquer anger by letting it subside before you speak or act. Anger might make you more vocal, but it never makes you truly powerful or effective.

THE PRESENT MOMENT

✦

Be Fully Alive

The present moment is a unique point in time—it will not come again. Rather than spending the here and now mulling over the past or fantasizing about the future, make a conscious decision to seize the moment. Now is the time to take action. Whether your goal is to travel the world, write a book, invent a time machine, or simply spend more time with your family, take the first step now.

A Meditation on Time

Time, it is said, is just nature's way of preventing everything from happening at once. Meditating on time can help us free ourselves from the tyranny of the clock. If we cling to experiences, we destroy them. The way to wholeness is to kiss each moment as it flies. Reflect on the nature of time without trying to resolve all its paradoxes.

"Reality is a stairway going neither down nor up. We do not move.
Today is today, always is today."
Octavio Paz (1914–1998)

Through the Window of the Present

Imagine yourself looking out through the window of the present—a peaceful scene of beautiful countryside stretches out before you. This is the land of all our tomorrows. In your mind's eye, open the window and let in the gentle winds of change. Try to sense the warm summer breeze brushing reassuringly against your cheeks. You can then let go of the past. There is nothing to fear from the future—embrace it with confidence.

Dissolving the Anchors

As we go about our daily business, our energies often become frayed or fragmented. While anticipating what the day holds in store for us, at the same time we hark back to yesterday—perhaps reprising a conversation with a friend or work colleague, or some triumph or disappointment we have undergone. These anchors keep us partly in the past. Bring yourself into the present by releasing every attachment that impedes your energy. Visualize the symbolic anchors dissolving, freeing you to be fully conscious of the moment, the here and now.

AWAKEN NOW

The Buddha said, "There is only one moment in time when it is essential to awaken. That moment is now." The only way to learn to fully appreciate the beauty of the world around us is to focus fully on the present moment. To be mentally absorbed in anything but the present is to be centered not in reality but in ideas *about* reality.

AFFIRMATION
I have everything I need for a full, rich, happy life.
My inner resources are abundant. I have plenty
of support.

WISDOM

◆

The All-Seeing Eye

The Eye of Horus is an ancient Egyptian symbol of the all-seeing eye, which pierces the illusion of the world around us. As humans we have a limited perception of reality. However, by properly looking, listening, thinking, and meditating, and by heeding our hearts as much as our minds, we can begin to perceive the world as it really is.

"The most beautiful emotion we can experience is the mystical. It is the power of all true art and science."
Albert Einstein (1879–1955)

The Wisdom of a Child

As adults we rarely allow ourselves to experience simple joys in the world as children do—dancing, for example, or closely observing an everyday phenomenon. Similarly, we forget that a child's wisdom often cuts straight to the heart of an issue. Go through a process of inner simplification. Try expressing your most troublesome dilemmas in language even a child would understand. Valuable insights may emerge from this technique.

A Book of Knowledge

Start a collection of favorite quotations—perhaps using an alphabetical notebook, with quotations entered under key themes such as Love, Spirit, Wisdom, and so on. You might start by classifying some of the quotations in this book. Read and listen widely—don't just restrict yourself to great literature or the writings of spiritual leaders. The wisest thoughts often come from unexpected sources—such as ordinary people acting courageously in a crisis.

Good Company

To read a book of spiritual wisdom is more than to absorb the lessons of the work—it is also to spend time in the enlightening company of a master. Try to sense the author's presence guiding you. Think of him or her as a trusted teacher, and enjoy privileged time shared with someone you admire.

"The superior man acquaints himself with many sayings of antiquity and many past deeds, in order to strengthen his character."

I Ching (c.300 BC)

60

YOUR THIRD EYE

Learn to trust your intuition. Visualize a point of light in the center of your forehead just above your eyes, like a radiating star. According to some traditions this is the position of your "third eye," the seat of intuition. Feel it radiating energy. Whenever you need strength or inspiration, call it to mind again and let it guide you.

61

Freedom of Thought

Seekers of wisdom, or of spiritual enlightenment, will seldom find fulfillment if they follow the herd instinct. Be bold enough to abandon popular ways of thinking if you find them unsatisfactory, and instead break out onto a new pathway of your own. Spiritual and intellectual freedom can be an exhilarating adventure.

"I like the silent church before the service begins better than any preaching."
Ralph Waldo Emerson (1803–1882)

A Commonplace Book

It is said that we can greatly enhance our quality of life by learning to improve our memory. But there's a shortcut— write things down! Keep a "commonplace book" with you —a notebook to record the best of what you read or hear. When you have a moment, reflect on your portable archive of personal wisdom—and let the most interesting thoughts sink into your consciousness. Don't worry if your book soon gets untidy—scribbles and corrections reflect the urgency of an alive intelligence.

CHAPTER 2

INSPIRING GOOD KARMA

Karma is the principle of returns—the spiritual law of cause and effect. This law holds that our behavior in this life dictates the level of being we will be born into in our next reincarnation. By extension, karma has come to signify the building of merit, or otherwise, within our own lifetime. We may not see the effects of our actions immediately, but they will inevitably return to us and enrich or impoverish our lives by accumulation.

This chapter suggests ways of working toward the best possible karma, by being fully aware of consequences. With good karma comes happiness.

"No act of kindness, however small, is ever wasted."
Aesop (620–560 BC)

ACTIONS & REACTIONS

♦

Goodness and Karma

Imagine that all your actions are like drops of rain falling on a pond. The ripples they make represent the signals you send out to the people around you. When the waves hit the bank, they turn and come back toward you. In the same way, if you send out goodness, you can expect kindness to come to you in return.

Wheels within Wheels

The turning of a windmill's sails might at first glance seem repetitive and meaningless. Yet the windmill is in fact making use of an elemental force—the wind—to be productive in an important task. Identify the repeated gestures of love you make in your life, the loving obligations you fulfill—for example, by working, by cooking, by giving support in a multitude of ways. Remember that each turn of the sails of love is a karmic dividend—an action that intensifies contentment.

HARVEST TIME

Good actions bring about a rich harvest—not just in the immediate, intended consequences, but also in more far-reaching effects that can ever be wholly perceived. For example, if you resolve that from now on you will respond to all situations, whether easy or difficult, with consideration for others and generosity of spirit, your behavior might inspire someone else to do the same. The harvest of virtue is always more abundant than it appears.

AFFIRMATION
I do all I can to relieve suffering in the world,
remembering to take care of myself so I can care
for others.

Personal Protection

Being aware of the karmic consequences of whatever you say or do can protect you from drifting toward bad karma. That does not mean that misfortune will always pass you by. But if it does come your way, you will gain strength from knowing that you have done your best for others.

"Let your hook be always cast. In the pool where you least expect it, will be fish."
Ovid (43 BC–17 AD)

LOVE & TRUST

✦

Trust Wisely

Trust is an essential ingredient in any close relationship. But often in life it will be necessary or desirable to trust someone with whom we do not have close ties—perhaps even a stranger. When investing trust in someone, do so wholeheartedly, without anxiety. Having made your trusting gesture, be true to it—as if it were a promise.

Heart and Soul

Our relationships with others often provide opportunities for growth and learning. Think about the person closest to you, what you value about them, and what you learn from them. Assess what they offer, both inside and outside your relationship. Karmic benefits come from giving others their due.

A Spiral of Loving Kindness

In the Tibetan loving kindness meditation you transmit loving feelings toward someone close to you, then you choose someone less close and send out love to them, then someone less close still, and so on, until you are including even people for whom you normally feel antipathy. Move outward like this, to stretch your capacity for love.

"Life has taught me that love does not consist in gazing at each other but in looking outward together in the same direction."
Antoine de Saint-Exupéry (1900–1944)

THE OPEN HEART

Visualize a butterfly in the center of your heart. It gently opens its wings, revealing its beauty. Breathe deeply and slowly, imagining each breath you take flowing into the butterfly, strengthening your love and compassion for it. After about five minutes, your heart will be more open to the world: free of inhibitions, it makes no exceptions.

"Love says: 'There is a way: I have traveled it thousands of times.'"
Rumi (1207–1273)

Let Them Fly

Be sure to let your loved ones have space to themselves from time to time—this is as important for your partner as it is for your children. When we try to tie someone down we are usually motivated by fear or insecurity. True love is not possessive—it allows the loved one to choose their own path. In a relationship based on love, trust, and respect, this path will never stray far from your own.

The Gift of the Heart

The commercialized extravaganza of Valentine's Day can distract us from its true symbolic meaning. As an antidote, celebrate your love for all your family and friends on this day. Also, whenever you are reminded of the occasion, send loving thoughts to someone dear to you, and say a prayer of thanks for them in your heart.

AFFIRMATION
From the infinite depth of my love I send powerful loving energies to all the friends of my heart.

Bridge to an Island

Visualize yourself as a floating island. Around you are other islands—all the people whose lives come close to yours, by choice or by chance. Pick an island that has only recently swum into view. Imagine throwing out a bridge and walking over to this new land. Who is the person? What is the bridge? Answer these questions and make your connection.

Spirit Mail

Imagine that your own spirit—the source of all love within yourself—has written a letter to a close friend, outlining why it persists with him or her, in a spirit of love, despite the various ups and downs of your relationship. What precisely would your spirit say? And how would your friend respond? Try answering these questions on paper, as a new stage in your journey toward good karma.

"Do not weep; do not wax indignant. Understand."
Baruch Spinoza (1632–1677)

FORGIVENESS

✦

HEALING GESTURES

It's important that you banish all resentment when someone has hurt you. Forgiveness is a matter of the heart, not
a ritual observance. However, reconciliation may come
more easily if you make a symbolic gesture—perhaps a
gift, an invitation, or some other action that resentment
would not allow.

A Memory of Sharing

Visualize reconciling your differences with someone you have fallen out with and can no longer see or talk to. Imagine that you are sharing a positive, joyful experience with this person, such as a walk in the park. Determine that, despite the breakdown in communication, you will go into the world as their friend, encountering that person in the happy memory of shared enjoyment.

GIVING

✦

Our True Purpose

Are you a superb cook, a good listener, a born organizer, or a great source of moral support? Spend a few moments taking stock of what you have to give others—whether practical or emotional, constructive, or empathetic. As long as we are ready to give, to share, and to love whenever the opportunity presents itself, we have a purpose. And with such a purpose we can never feel lost or alone.

" Thousands of candles can be lighted from a single candle, and the life of the candle will not be shortened. Happiness never decreases by being shared."
The Buddha (c.563–c.483 BC)

Esteem Your Guests

Next time you invite guests for lunch or dinner, why not show your appreciation of them by leaving a little present on each of their places at table? This should be a token of your love for them, and therefore a symbolic item, rather than an expensive gift. You could, for example, leave a fresh flower on each plate, or write down a happy wish on decorative paper. Because they show thoughtfulness, such small gestures can bring karmic dividends.

Generous Giving

Give your best, not what's left over. When the value of a gift is too carefully assessed by the giver, generosity is diminished. To give well is to give without thought of the cost, or of a sense of sacrifice—and take pleasure in the recipient's joy. Err on the side of excess.

"From the infinitely changeless vessel of spirit, I savor the inexhaustible richness of generosity."
Eduardo Cuadro (1820–1903)

SHARE YOUR SKILLS

Sharing skills or labor within the community is a great way to strengthen friendships and save cash. This is the "favors bank." Some local networks might even go as far as to issue checkbooks to facilitate such exchanges of skills. However, most people prefer a less formal approach. Start by offering your services gratis: The law of karma will soon start to take effect.

Teach a Skill

One of life's most rewarding activities is imparting a skill to others. This can be anything from origami, to wind-surfing, to ballroom dancing. Identify your greatest skill and take double pleasure in exercising a talent and passing it on, if only by example, to someone else.

AFFIRMATION

None of my special talents is mine alone. I offer them freely. I am happy to see others surpass me.

Be a Neighborhood Host

Ask neighbors around to your place for suppers that combine good food and hospitality with debate about issues of local concern—or perhaps simply an exchange of news and views. To know your neighbors well is to be well-rooted in your local community. This can give you both a source of support and an opportunity to give something back to the people you live among.

The Open Heart

An open heart symbolizes one of the highest of all spiritual precepts—the path of service. If we think of ourselves as here to perform selfless deeds, however small, for other people, we gain in spiritual stature and well-being. Think of your heart as a mobile dispensary of largesse, permanently open for anyone who calls upon its services.

"And the day came when the risk to remain tight in a bud was more painful than the risk it took to blossom."
Anaïs Nin (1903–1977)

Against Waste

We all know that wasting things can be irresponsible. It is wrong to squander wealth, or food, or resources of any kind, when there are so many in need. But how many of us think, before we throw something away, whether it might be useful to someone else? Make a habit of considering this question and acting upon it. And be similarly intolerant of wasting the time you could be using for other people's benefit.

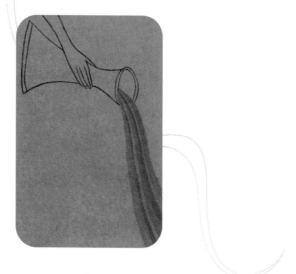

G R A T I T U D E

✦

At Home in Your Life

Sit quietly and reflect on your life right now. It is changing. The future is unknown: Some of your hopes will not
be realized—but neither will some of your fears. You are
on a journey, moving in a landscape that itself is in flux.
Take a moment to appreciate where you are now in your
life ... and feel gratitude for the sense of being "at home."

The Five Great Blessings

The Chinese believe we each have five great blessings:
Happiness, health, virtue, peace, and longevity. Take one
week, and on each day, focus on one of these qualites.
On Monday, bring happiness to yourself and family. On
Tuesday, eat healthily, and exercise for at least twenty
minutes. On Wednesday, make an effort to spread kindness. On Thursday, meditate on peace for ten minutes.
The fifth blessing, longevity, comes from wealth in the
others. On Friday, give thanks for this wealth. At the
weekend, weave all the blessings in a tapestry of spirit,
and give thanks for this too.

REPEATED PLEASURES

A child on a carousel often wishes the ride would last forever. Some adult pastimes elicit the same feeling—such as cooking a meal for friends or walking in your favorite park. Enjoy one of these familiar pleasures; ask yourself what made it so special. If you can summon up two or three answers, you may come closer to the secret of what is so wonderful about being alive.

"Friendship runs dancing through the world bringing to us all the summons to awake and sing its praises."
Epicurus (341–270 BC)

Pools of Insight

Consider all the people who have been sources of insight in your life. Perhaps you have been inspired by a teacher, a mentor, a friend, or a relative. Try to make regular contact with these sources—your own personal pools of wisdom. Take time to think about and cherish the gifts that each pool has given to you.

"You are an ocean of knowledge hidden in a dew drop."
Rumi (1207–1273)

The Beauty of the Ordinary

You can discover an aspect of gratitude in the most mundane chores if you approach them with an enlightened mind. For example, while sweeping away fallen leaves, think of the beauty and majesty of the trees that shed them. Reflect on the eternal cycle of the seasons and give thanks to the earth for sustaining life.

Multiplicity

A pomegranate, sliced in half, is an inspiring symbol of life's diversity. Use it to come to terms with people who think or behave differently from you. Imagine that the countless seeds are all different approaches people can take to life. Meditate on the multiplicity of the pomegranate, in gratitude that humanity is so varied.

CREATIVITY

✦

Catch the Thought

Our thoughts are a stream—most of them rush past our consciousness. We tend to treat all these passing thoughts as outtakes, or useless imaginings, but sometimes, in abandoning such thoughts, we are throwing away something valuable. Like an artist creating art from what other people might jettison, salvage good ideas from bad.

"Time is but the stream I go a-fishing in."
Henry David Thoreau (1817–1862)

Sharing Song

You don't have to play an instrument to be able to enjoy music creatively—you can use your voice. Singing alone is invigorating and cathartic, but singing with others brings even more benefits. Join a choir and you'll improve your teamwork and listening skills, experience the exhilaration of live performance, and gain access to a great repertoire of choral music, from classical to gospel.

Refreshing Adventure

Novelty for its own sake is not a sound principle on which to base a life—we need continuity to grow and form bonds with others. However, it is good to have an ingredient of adventure in the mix. Whether through travel or meeting new people, push the boundaries of your experience—you will find it stimulating and refreshing.

AFFIRMATION

I take delight in all the possibilities around me.
I enjoy life fully and with gratitude.

CREATIVE WRITING

If you've never tried your hand at creative writing, why not experiment a little? Perhaps try a "stream-of-consciousness" approach, just spending half an hour seeing what brain and pen (or keyboard) will produce when freed from formal or rational constraints. You never know, your noodling might become a basis for a short story or poem. Give it a try, and see what happens.

CONNECTIONS

✦

Shared Experience

Like a shoal of fish swimming as one within the ocean, humankind is bound together by a common destiny. While finding your own path in life, draw strength from the knowledge that everyone around you is also on a journey. You are never wholly alone: others experience similar trials and similar triumphs.

"Love is infallible; it has not errors, for all errors are the want of love."
Andrew Bonar Law (1858–1923)

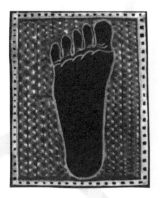

A Footprint in the Sand

Imagine you are marooned on a tropical island that you assume is uninhabited. Then one day, like Robinson Crusoe, you find a footprint in the sand. Who might have made this print? What might you expect to learn from him or her? Imagine what you in return would have to offer. How would you connect with this person, without the benefit of language? An imaginative exercise of this kind can help you come to a closer understanding of what you need from other people, and why you might be important to them, too.

Changing Selves

If you're experiencing difficulties in a relationship, try switching roles to resolve the issue. Act out a dialogue in which you each take the other's viewpoint, to dramatize your partner's concerns as you imagine them—especially resentments, doubts, and insecurities. Surprising revelations may emerge, pointing the way to a solution.

At Your Own Pace

When talking to someone about things that matter, always remember that you needn't follow the pace of the other person's thinking. Pause for as long as you like, and think things through. Speak as slowly as you like. The right thoughts and words sometimes take time to organize themselves.

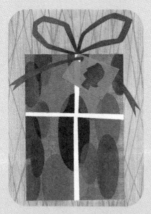

THE GIFT OF ANOTHER

Meeting new people is often like receiving a gift-wrapped present. Many of their special qualities will be hidden from your sight at first meeting, so be persistent. You need to unpeel the wrapping to discover what's inside—everyone has surprises to offer that only show themselves on closer acquaintance.

"The greatest good you can do for another is not just to share your riches but to reveal to him his own."
Benjamin Disraeli (1804–1881)

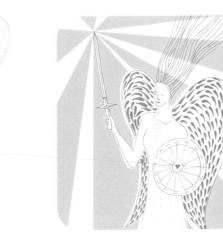

Truth Telling

Sometimes it's in a friend's best interests that you tell them the truth, even though you know they will find it difficult to accept. When you sense that this is your duty, steel yourself—do not backtrack to make your role easier. Choose your words carefully. True friendship takes such challenges in its stride.

Avoiding Mirages

It is easy to drift into delusion, which can show as low self-esteem or its opposite, self-importance. Avoid this snare by talking freely and honestly among your family and friends. Ask them from time to time if you're right— and heed them if they say you're not!

"Between whom there is hearty truth, there is love."
Henry David Thoreau (1817–1862)

Solitary Adventure

The unencumbered spirit on a voyage doesn't feel daunted by solitude, but regards it as a privilege—just as company and love are privileges. Seek moments of solitude in your life—afterwards, you'll appreciate your loved ones all the more.

Bright Futures

Spend an evening with friends taking turns telling each other's fortunes. Each "fortune teller" should practice kindness and generosity toward the subject by imagining the best possible future for them, considering both material and spiritual aspects.

AFFIRMATION

I am co-creating a world of peace, caring, and goodwill. No matter what happens, I choose to be a channel of love.

EMBRACING COMMUNITY

In the pursuit of our personal goals it is easy to forget that we belong to the extended family that is our local community. Try to make time for your neighbors: Visit their homes if you can and try to imagine how things look from their perspective. Consider getting together with them to help organize a street party, or perhaps a meal out in a new local restaurant.

KINDNESS & COMPASSION

Cultivate Empathy

When we see the hole in one half of a cut-open avocado, we immediately know what has caused it—the stone. In the same way a person who shows empathy intuitively understands the signs that other people show in their behavior and speech, and offers compassion accordingly. Cultivate empathy—the art of putting yourself in another person's place.

"What do we live for if not to make life less difficult for each other?"
George Eliot (1819–1880)

A Feather's Weight

We affect others in many ways: the smallest action or utterance can have great effect. Imagine a feather in your open hands, held up close to your mouth while you speak. The feather would flutter and lift on the currents of your breath. Be careful not to upset anyone unwittingly by thoughtless talk. Use empathy to anticipate possible reactions to what you say.

Practical Empathy

If you know somebody who is under serious stress or in difficult circumstances, the kindest thing you can do may be to give practical help—perhaps by doing an errand. You may even help incognito, without anyone discovering what you've done. Think and feel yourself into this person's situation and act accordingly—this is true empathy.

Acts of Kindness

According to Confucius, kindness is one of the essential virtues, yet many of us do not realize its full potential. The word itself is significant: by showing kindness, we give full recognition to others of our own kind. In this way, we emphasize our interconnectedness. Every day perform at least one genuinely kind act—either practical or symbolic.

"True compassion flows fast, as if we were wounded ourselves,
yet without diminishing our strength."
Haruki Mishimi (1908–1991)

EYES OF COMPASSION

In the Buddhist tradition, the one hundred eyes on a peacock's tail symbolize compassionate watchfulness. Watch over others and feel compassion for their sufferings. The Dalai Lama has said that if we have a good heart and warm feelings, we will be able to achieve contentment, and will have the power to radiate a peaceful atmosphere. Compassionate watchfulness is second nature to the enlightened spirit.

The Jewel in the Lotus

Awaken your compassion by meditating on Avalokiteshvara, the embodiment of the Buddha's compassion. His mantra is *Om Mani Padme Hum,* which means "the jewel in the lotus"—the treasure within ourselves. Calm your mind with some gentle breathing and think about the suffering experienced by everybody, including yourself. Softly chant this mantra and open your heart to compassion.

"I will cease to live as a self and will take as my self
my fellow creatures."
Shantideva (8th century AD)

Message in a Bottle

Traditionally, a castaway will launch a message in a bottle in the hope that it will drift across the sea to reach a potential rescuer. Such messages are often sent out, in a metaphorical sense, by people we know—people who are perhaps wary of asking for help directly, so they make a coded plea. Look out for these muted cries for help, and respond to them sensitively and caringly—your friends and family may be in greater need of help than they are prepared to admit.

Understanding Our Friends

Trying to understand someone who is very different from you is the first step in showing them compassion. When dealing with friends, however, we might imagine that their needs are much the same as ours. Make sensitive inquiries on this point. Sometimes our friends have surprisingly different priorities.

The Gift of Listening

When we focus wholeheartedly on another's words we are both giving and receiving. Be sure to listen well to anyone who has a problem to share with you. Pay attention to the tone of voice and to the silences between words, as well as to the words themselves. You are performing a positive kindness even if you offer no advice. Do not judge what you hear. If you choose to speak, say nothing negative—repeating a simple positive message is better than saying something too elaborate or clever.

THE BELL AND THE THUNDERBOLT

In Tantric Buddhism the vajra, or thunderbolt, is the compassion of the Buddha, the active principle; while the bell is wisdom, the passive principle. To achieve enlightenment, the two are combined. In your dealings with others, do not be wise without compassion, nor compassionate without wisdom.

AFFIRMATION
I will have compassion for the weaknesses I see in others—reflecting compassion for the weaknesses I see in myself.

107

Be a Well

When people in need make demands upon your energies, visualize yourself as a well that gets replenished from a natural underground spring—symbolizing the bottomless desire you have to give service to others. Affirm to yourself that your own love is infinite—it will be never be exhausted by the demands placed upon it.

"Have compassion on those you can see, and He whom you cannot see will have compassion on you."
Hadith (7th century AD)

Love for a Stranger

Take a map of the world and choose a place at random. Imagine yourself in a satellite above the Earth with a powerful telescope. In your mind's eye, zoom in on the place you have chosen until you visualize just one individual going about their business. Send this person rays of love. All people are your kin, equally deserving of your love and compassion.

109

◆

Cutting the Chain of Blame

We often feel tempted to pass on blame to someone else in apparent vindication of ourselves—even though at least some of the fault may lie at our own door. In this way we risk initiating a "chain of blame." It is always more constructive to cut the chain, even if it means admitting to more responsibility than we feel in the situation.

The Peacemaker's Breakthrough

It is all too easy after a quarrel to feel aggrieved and refuse on principle to make up—especially if you believe that you are not at fault. However, it is good to be a peacemaker: All it takes is to step out of the tit-for-tat mentality, show a little courage, and make a generous gesture. You will not regret it.

"The weak can never forgive. Forgiveness is the attribute of the strong."
Mahatma Gandhi (1869–1948)

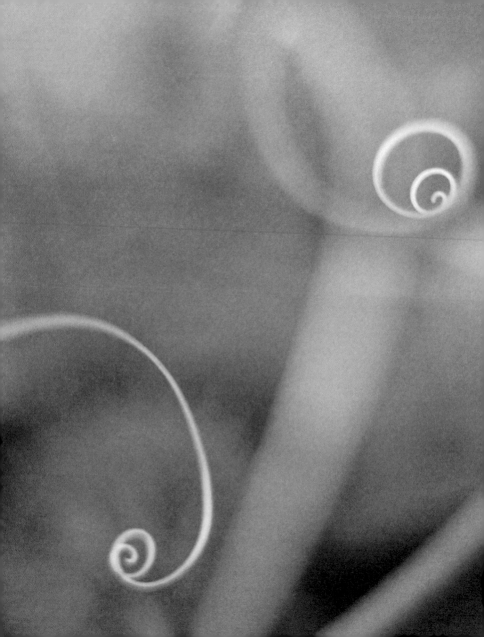

CHAPTER 3

INSPIRING THE BODY

We obtain energy for life from food, clean water, fresh air, exercise, and sleep. These are things we enjoy every day and often take for granted, but from time to time—perhaps at the start of each new season of the year—we can benefit from a program of self-renewal to bring our energy levels up to speed.

This chapter will show you how to revitalize yourself, covering diet and detox, rest and relaxation, exercise and fitness, ways to get your chi (vital energy) moving, and many other aspects of improving your physical health.

"The human body is vapor, materialized by sunshine and mixed with the life of the stars."
Paracelsus (1493–1541)

THE BODY'S ENERGY

A Ball of Energy

In Indian philosophy, the life-force we breathe in is called prana. The Chinese call it chi. To feel its energy, stand with legs apart, your hands in front of your abdomen, palms facing each other. Imagine your hands encircling a ball of energy emanating from below your navel. Your fingers may tingle, or your hands may feel warm.

"The eye by which I see God is the same eye by which God sees me."
Meister Eckhart (1260–1327)

Shiatsu for Stress

"Connection shiatsu" can relieve short, shallow breathing caused by stress. Lie on your back and place the palm of one hand on your abdomen, the palm of the other on your chest. Hold for one minute. This will stimulate the flow of chi between your lungs and your kidneys (the "seat" of anxiety), helping you to relax and breathe more deeply.

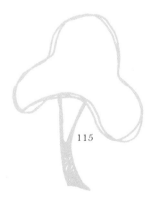

115

Fire Breathing

The Kundalini practice of fire breathing raises chi, and is said to oxygenate the blood, cleanse the organs, and tone the system. Take a long, deep breath, filling your lungs. Exhale in quick snorts, as if blowing your nose, while rapidly contracting and releasing your stomach muscles. Continue for one or two minutes, stopping sooner if you experience any dizziness or discomfort.

Unblock Your Throat Chakra

Working with your chakras (energy centers, in the Indian tradition) helps balance your body's energy and harmonize your mental, physical, and spiritual well-being. Visualize a spinning blue disk at the front of your throat. This will help to unblock your throat chakra, soothing stress and improving communication through speech.

AFFIRMATION
I am healthy, fit, and full of energy. I allow my body to absorb only what is nourishing. I radiate joy.

PEACEFUL PRESSURES

Acupressure uses thumb pressure or fingertip massage to relax physical tensions. The acupoint located just below the ball of your foot, a third of the way along the sole, is used to relieve fatigue and to boost vitality. Sit with your right foot on your left knee. Apply pressure to the acupoint with your right thumb for two minutes. Repeat on your left foot.

Renew Yourself with Yoga

During inverted yoga postures, blood rushes toward the head, bathing the brain in oxygen, and revitalizing both body and spirit. Lie on your back and lean your legs against a wall. Lightly clasp your hands above your head, on the floor, your arms forming a diamond. Breathe deeply and evenly. Done for 10 minutes before bedtime, this will promote restful sleep.

The Point of a Sword

Amergin, the great Irish magician, one day announced: "I am the point of a sword." He could lose himself in an action as if by magic. When attempting a difficult activity, concentrate your whole attention on what you want to achieve. Banish distraction. Become the point of a sword.

"Be resolved and the thing is done."
Chinese proverb

DIET & DETOX

◆

Know Your Food

Diet fads come and go, but the essentials of good nutrition remain the same. Limit your intake of saturated fats, sugar, and additives; make sure you eat enough fiber, essential fats, vitamins, and minerals. If all this sounds technical, don't be deterred: Eating well is a basic life skill. Learn it and make it second nature.

Food for Thought

Breakfast is the most important meal of the day as it ends your overnight fast and provides energy for the rest of the day. You will benefit most from healthy, nutrient-rich foods, such as fruit or oatmeal, and if you eat more in the morning than in the evening you will feel energetic during the day and find it easier to fall asleep at night.

"Bad habits are easier to abandon today than tomorrow."
Yiddish proverb

INNER CLEANSING

When we are under stress, toxins build up in our bodies. Redress the balance by undertaking a raw-food or juice diet for one or two days. When short of calories, the body first metabolizes old or diseased tissues, so this diet constitutes an effective spring-clean. Drink at least four pints of pure spring water each day, and rest as much as you need. Try this regime over a quiet weekend at home and see how it revives both body and spirit.

Healthy Elixirs

Get to know your herbal teas: try a new one each week and explore the vast variety of tastes. Each tea has beneficial qualities: camomile and barley are calming; dandelion, pear, and apple detoxify; St. John's wort releases aches and pains. Discover which is the right tea for you.

Crystal Power

Some people use crystals to help absorb low-level electro-magnetic radiation produced by computer and TV screens. Experts claim that the most effective crystals for this purpose are Smoky Quartz and Black Tourmaline. Place a crystal on or near the screen. According to traditional crystal lore, its energies will reduce the damage caused by electromagnetic "smog."

"Nature is the art of God."
Dante Alighieri (1265–1321)

SLEEP, REST & RELAXATION

◆

A Peaceful Night

Sleep is nature's restorative. To ensure a good, restful night, avoid caffeine for at least four hours before going to bed. Add a few drops of lavender oil to a warm bath, or drink a cup of relaxing camomile or valerian tea. If, in the night, you lie awake worrying, jot down a list of issues on a sheet of paper, and leave them to the morning.

The Sleep Experiment

Go to bed when tired but not exhausted. Note the time. Listen to gentle music, read a soothing book, or meditate just before sleep. Don't set your alarm; allow yourself to wake naturally. How long did you sleep? Repeat this exercise every night until your sleep pattern becomes regular. This is your natural and most restful sleep cycle.

"Knock on the sky and listen to the sound."
Zen saying

HERBAL HELP

If you have trouble falling asleep, try using a herbal pillow. Fill a small fabric bag with lavender, orange peel, and cloves. Put in therapeutic herbs such as hops, valerian, or peppermint. Add a few drops of vegetable oil and tie up the bag. Place it underneath your pillow. Let its fragrances waft you to sleep.

AFFIRMATION

As I fall asleep I entrust my body's care to the benevolent spirit of the cosmos, grateful for a period of deep renewal.

Under the Stars

Sleeping outside in summer—in a tent or on the veranda—is an novel way to experience the living world beyond the bubble of the home. Even city-dwellers will find a rich nighttime tapestry of sounds and smells, while in the country there are lovely perfumes and the uplifting spectacle of the stars.

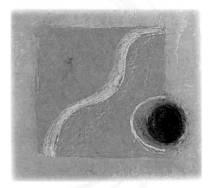

Blissful Bed

Our bed plays a crucial role in the quality of our sleep, so it pays to invest in a good-quality one. Take time when choosing a new bed, and don't be pressurized by over-enthusiastic salespeople. Always look for comfort and the level of support that's right for you. When trying out a bed in the store, take off your shoes, and lie on the bed in your usual sleeping position for at least ten minutes.

"Happiness is the absence of striving for happiness."
Chuang Tzu (c.350–c.286 BC)

A Japanese Garden

The Japanese are skilled in creating gardens of exceptional beauty and tranquility with enduring water, rock, and evergreens, rather than transient flowers. Conjure up an imaginary Japanese garden as a "virtual" sanctuary whenever you need a few minutes' relief from worldly stresses.

Sea Tumbling

A good relaxation exercise is to immerse yourself in the vastness of an imaginary sea and let its power cleanse you of anxiety. This exercise works well for those who find visualization difficult: All you need to do is conjure the feeling of the sea and its turbulent energy. As an ancient Tibetan Buddhist text tells us, the aim is "to swim within the energies of the senses."

"Knowing what is enough is wealth."
Lao Tzu (c.604–531 BC)

INNER CLOCK

We all tend to live by the artificial sense of time that clocks impose. Choose one day, as soon as possible, when you organize your schedule according to your inner clock. Exercise when you are restless, eat when you are hungry, and rest when you feel tired. Relax and enjoy the luxury of tuning into your natural rhythms. And remember— don't wear your watch!

Mindful Relaxation

Anyone who has set themselves on the path to spiritual maturity might be tempted to feel that pure relaxation is an indulgence. But we all need to unwind. Take the opportunity to relax whenever you feel you have done enough to deserve it. Try to appreciate the joy of each passing moment. Relaxing can be a spiritual exercise if approached in a spirit of mindfulness.

Retreat and Renew

Go on a mini-retreat for a morning, an afternoon, or an entire day. Ban the phone, the TV and radio, and the car—unless you need the car to reach your chosen place of retreat. Meditate and give thanks for your blessings. Mindfully appreciate the moment.

"Only in solitude do we find ourselves."
Miguel de Unamuno (1864–1936)

131

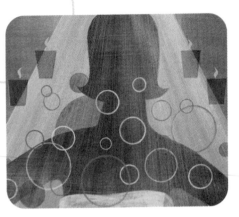

Enjoy a Herbal Bath

At the end of the day, enjoy a warm bath to the full by adding herbs to make it a truly relaxing experience. Camomile, which has sedative properties, can be particularly effective. Infuse two teaspoonfuls of the herb in boiling water and leave the mixture to stand for ten minutes. Then pour it through a strainer into your bath water.

Flower Remedies

Dr Bach's flower remedies were formulated to help conditions as diverse as exhaustion, guilt, and despair. The energy of thirty-eight different plants are captured in individual essences—and often you need only drink a few drops in water to benefit from their soothing properties.

"Little flower, but if I could understand, what you are, root and all in all, I should know what God and man is."
Alfred Lord Tennyson (1809–1892)

T O U C H

✦

Close Contact

Human touch has a very special quality. Nothing comforts a baby as quickly or effectively as its mother's hug, and even someone you don't know well can convey many things—empathy, or condolence, or solidarity—with a simple touch. Explore the warmth of touch with someone you love. Connect with the universal life-force.

Practice Stroking

Stroking is the simplest form of massage—you need to master it before you can move on to more complex techniques. Practice on your partner or a friend. Concentrate on making your movements flowing and rhythmic, and experiment with speed and pressure to add variety.

AFFIRMATION

I explore experience with all my senses — my portals to the world outside myself. For each of them I give my heartfelt thanks.

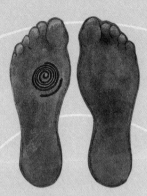

FOOT MASSAGE

A gentle foot massage can leave you feeling rejuvenated.
Try simple thumb circles. Support the heel of your partner's foot in one hand and wrap the other hand around so
that the pad of your thumb rests on the ball of the foot.
Slowly rotate your thumb in small circles. Applying a little pressure, work all around and below the ball of the
foot. Repeat on the other foot.

Kneading and Percussion

As you become more confident at massaging, experiment with kneading—a technique whereby you press the flesh firmly with the fingers, as though kneading dough. This is ideal for releasing tension in the shoulders and fleshy areas of the body. At the end of massage use percussion movements to energize the person. Either form your hands into loose fists and bounce them alternately against the skin, or strike the skin with the sides of your hands.

"Never hesitate to hold out your hand; never hesitate to accept the outstretched hand of another."
Pope John XXIII (1881–1963)

136

Neck Massage

Be kind to your neck. The neck and shoulders are often the first areas to tense up under stress, leading to headaches and neck strain. Roll your head slowly from side to side and up and down to help release the tightness, and ask your partner or a friend to massage the back of your neck and between your shoulder blades—relax and let the tension disappear.

Back Massage

Massaging the back, where the spinal nerves governing many of the body's functions are situated, can benefit the whole body—and when combined with aromatherapy oils, the mind, too. Blend 4 drops lavender oil, 4 drops mandarin, and 2 drops sandalwood in 4 tsp sweet almond oil for a truly luxurious and relaxing experience.

Hand Massage

Exchange a loving hand massage with a friend. Begin by stroking the center of the back of one of their hands with both of your thumbs. Make circular movements over the palm with your thumbs; then soothingly stroke from fingertips to palm with your fist. Squeeze gently several times along each finger. Finish by stroking the back of the hand again.

"If anything is sacred, the human body is sacred."
Walt Whitman (1819–1892)

EARTH ENERGY

Draw strength from Mother Earth. Collect a handful of
pebbles in your hand and lightly play with them. Feel
their smoothness and listen to the sound they make as
they click against each other. Imagine the earth they have
been lying in for thousands of years. Tap into the vast
powers that created our planet.

SOOTHING THE FACE

◆

A Face Massage for Stress Relief

Release tension by doing this face massage on yourself. Using your index and middle fingers, make circles on your brow, moving from the center outward toward your temples. Then make sharp upward strokes along the bridge of your nose. Finally, close your eyes and gently rest the heels of your hands on your eye sockets. Do each of these three stages for about a minute.

Drawing the Face

How well do you know yourself? Most of us find it hard to close our eyes and create a vivid mental picture of our face. You can give your face a massage and sharpen this mental image at the same time by running your fingers over your face with your eyes closed. Once the image is crystal-clear in your mind, the massage is complete.

AFFIRMATION

I accept myself completely as I am today. Aging is natural. I am committed to my inner unfolding.

Inner Light

Just as stress and worry are reflected in your face, so too are inner calm and serenity. Grant yourself a little time each day to spend in meditation. Think about yourself, acknowledging honestly what you've done well and where there is room for improvement. Endeavor to be at peace with who you are, and you will soon discover that you shine with an inner light—it's more effective than any beauty product!

A Lavender Infusion

Enjoy a facial infused with lavender to soothe away stress. Place a handful of dried lavender in a pan of water, bring to the boil, and then simmer for ten minutes. Remove from the stove and place on a heat-resistant surface. Hold your head over the water under a towel "tent" for about five minutes. Then rinse your face with cool water.

"All things are artificial, for nature is the art of God."
Sir Thomas Browne (1605–1682)

BREATH

✦

Develop Breath Awareness

By becoming more aware of our breathing we can consciously alter its pattern to make ourselves more relaxed. Lie on your back with eyes closed, breathing through your nose. Place one hand on your chest and one on your abdomen, and focus on your hands as they rise and fall, reflecting the rhythm and depth of your breathing.

The Isle of Calm

When we are anxious, our breathing becomes shallow and rapid. To calm yourself, imagine that you are lying on a beach on a tropical island. You can hear waves gently lapping against the shore. Listen to your in-breaths and out-breaths, then try to synchronize them with the sound of the waves. As your breathing slows and deepens, you will automatically relax.

"Take the breath of the new dawn and make it part of you.
It will give you strength."
Hopi saying

AROMA-SOOTHING

Isolate a few smells in nature that you find calming—perhaps the scent of a rose or the smell of freshly mown grass. Select one that can be made available to you. Sit or lie quietly, focusing on the smell to amplify it in your perception. Breathing deeply, think of the aroma as a relaxant that draws you into the center of your being with every inhalation. Exhale your stress.

Profound Breathing

Correct breathing is essential to the flow of chi around the body, which in turn affects both our physical and emotional well-being. Spend ten minutes each day breathing purposefully from the diaphragm rather than from the chest—as you do so, your abdomen should rise and fall. Breathing in this way gives maximum ventilation in the lower part of the lungs and makes you feel relaxed in body and mind.

Sun Breath

This is a deep breathing technique that relieves tension. It is essentially one breath, in three stages. Stand with hands by your sides. Breathe into your belly while stretching out your arms. Then breathe into the mid-chest as you bring your hands into a prayer position at your heart. Next, lift them above over your head as you breathe into your upper chest. As you exhale, lower your hands to your sides.

"When the breath is irregular, the mind is also unsteady; but when the breath is still, so is the mind."
Hathayogapradipika (14th century)

7/11 Breath Control

To calm yourself when in an agitated state, breathe in slowly and steadily to the count of seven. Then breathe out slowly and steadily to the count of eleven. Continue with this rhythm until you become more relaxed and the tension that triggered your anxiety begins to subside.

Incense Magic

Burning aromatic oils and resins is an age-old method of enhancing or inducing a mood. Invest in a small incense burner and choose different fragrances for different purposes: Peppermint or bergamot to increase energy; ylang-ylang to evoke a romantic atmosphere; camomile or juniper to release tension; mandarin, neroli, or sandalwood to calm the mind; and geranium or lavender to bring harmony and balance.

"One touch of nature makes the whole world kin."
William Shakespeare (1564–1616)

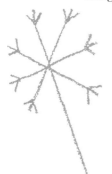

CEREMONIAL BATHTIME

Many ancient ceremonies included a ritual bath, whose purpose was not to cleanse the body but to prepare the spirit for transformation. In the evening, before meditating or performing a personal rite, draw a deep bath. Light candles in your bathroom and burn frankincense essential oil, which helps still the mind and calm the breath. As you bathe, allow the water to wash away all thoughts of the day, to deepen your connection to the spirit.

A Singing Heart

Singing is good for relaxation, and good for your health, since it encourages deep breathing and releases energy. It's also an excellent way to break down boundaries: Complete strangers who come together to sing soon find that their love of music and of singing leads them to find more common ground and shared enthusiasms.

The Healing Sun

The Celts celebrated the energy-giving sun and its healing powers on the longest day of the year, the Summer Solstice. Mark the actual day by watching the sunrise, ideally from a hilltop with a good view over city or countryside. Enjoy the ritual, a symbolic moment of unparalleled brilliance.

"The earth has received the embrace of the sun and we shall see the results of that love."
Chief Sitting Bull (c.1831–1890)

Enjoy the Elements

It's easy to have fun outside when it's warm and sunny, but try not to let bad weather keep you inside. See rain and wind as a challenge to get out there and let nature bring a glow to your cheeks. If you make a habit of healthy walking whatever the weather, you'll be surprised how often the heavens smile on you.

Releasing Sadness

Whenever you feel sad, take yourself for a walk. Focus your attention on whatever you see as you pass. It doesn't matter where you go or how often you follow the same path. With each step, you dislodge negative feelings and open yourself positively to sights, sounds, and smells.

AFFIRMATION
I am at play in the world. Everything I experience
fills me with delight. My greatest pleasure is
spreading joy.

WALKING TALL

Practice walking with awareness, whether you are on your way to the local store or bus-stop or taking some fresh air in the park. Begin by feeling your feet make contact with the ground, then notice every time you raise each foot and plant it down again. Walk with dignity and awareness, and enjoy walking for its own sake. You will soon find that a profound sense of peaceful well-being begins to permeate your consciousness.

153

EXERCISE & FITNESS

Stretch for Joy

Start your day with a simple stretching routine. Reach your arms up to the sky and then stretch out first one and then the other arm. Revel in how your whole body lengthens and loosens. Then stretch each part of your body in turn, gently at first, starting with the feet and working up, and making sure that you keep breathing deeply and regularly. You will soon feel fully awake.

Unwind Like a Cat

Relieve tension by stretching like a cat. First, stand as straight and tall as you can. Next, loosely roll your neck, shoulders, arms, and wrists. Sit on the floor with your legs in front of you and rotate your ankles. With your hands, lift first one knee, then the other, bringing each one close to your chest. See how much freer you feel.

"The body is a sacred garment ... it is what you enter life in and what you depart life with, and it should be treated with honor."
Martha Graham (1894–1991)

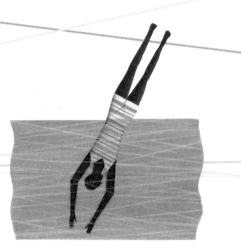

In the Swim

Swimming strengthens the body and heart, soothes the mind, regulates breathing, and stimulates the circulation—all without putting stress on the joints. And the regular movements of swimming give it a calming quality. Try to build swimming into your weekly routine.

"Now may every living thing, young or old, weak or strong, living near or far, known or unknown, living or departed or yet unborn, may every living thing be full of bliss."
The Buddha (c.563–c.483 BC)

Power Walking

You don't have to go to a costly gym to get fit. Instead try introducing a power walk into your daily or weekly routine to help you keep in shape. Start with short walks about 10 minutes long. Walk faster than normal, and swing your arms. Time yourself to measure performance and keep up motivation. Your aim is to walk for at least 20 minutes at a speed of around 5 mph (average walking speed is 3 mph). You'll soon start to enjoy these power walks and build them happily into your day.

AT HOME
& AT WORK

◆

The Spirit of Home

A home is more than just bricks and mortar and a roof over our heads—it's where we spend an important part of our lives, express our love for our family, and feel we can relax and be ourselves. Decorating your own home will imbue it with your personality and make it somewhere that resonates with warmth and welcome.

At the Threshold

The threshold of your home should set the tone appropriate to a place of refuge and peace. Near the door, on the outside wall, you could hang some wind chimes, or a plaque inscribed with the Chinese character for longevity or abundance. These will remind you to unwind whenever you come home.

AFFIRMATION
Peace begins at home. When I come from a place of
inner peace, I see peace around me.

DECLUTTER NOW

According to feng shui, clutter in the home creates an environment in which energy stagnates. Choose a room or a part of a room that feels overcrowded, and recycle or dispose of everything for which you no longer have a use. Clearing clutter allows chi (spiritual energy) to flow around the home more readily. You will be conscious of this profound improvement the moment you walk into the room—even if all the clutter you have cleared away was hidden within storage spaces.

The Art of Placement

Follow esthetic principles of harmony and balance when arranging objects in your home. Largely intuitive, these relate to grouping pieces by color tones, sizes, and textures. Adjust your arrangement until it feels just right, removing anything that fights the mood. Harmony of this kind will subtly relax you whenever you are in the room.

Household Energy

Learn about the ancient Indian practice of vastu—a distant cousin of feng shui. The relationship of a house's different features and the arrangement of details such as candles and mirrors can beneficially alter the natural flow of energy around the home.

"Unless the Lord builds the house, its builders labor in vain."
Psalms 127:1

Pineapple Day

In the Caribbean, sea captains used to place a pineapple, symbol of hospitality, on their gatepost as a sign that they had returned from their voyages and were now welcoming visitors. Consider having a "pineapple day" at home, when all your friends are welcome. Pineapple, of course, must be on the menu!

The Random Concert

Sit by an open window and listen to the sounds you hear. The traffic, the construction, are all part of a vast symphony you are privileged to witness. Imagine the good outcomes—an ambulance rushing to someone's aid, a new hotel going up with views over the park. Take pleasure in the noise around you, instead of being irritated by it.

"If you have knowledge, let others light their candles at it."
Margaret Fuller (1810–1850)

THE SPECTRUM
OF MEANING

The colors we use to decorate our homes can influence our moods and affect our well-being. When choosing colors for a room, instead of simply picking those that you find pleasing to the eye, consider also their spiritual symbolism. Red conveys passionate conviction; orange, spiritual endeavor; yellow, optimism; green, nature and harmony; blue, openness; indigo, mystery; and violet, spiritual vision.

Reflecting Ourselves

Our living spaces can be seen as a reflection of our inner world, our values. By changing the outer world, we can even work changes within ourselves. Awaken to the reassuring truth that your home can be a sanctuary, a refuge from the world's demands. Make it a beautiful place to be, and somewhere fit to satisfy the demands of the spirit.

"All the way to heaven is heaven."
St. Catherine of Siena (1347–1380)

Inspiring Words

Make your home a place of time-honored wisdom. Find thought-provoking quotations—you could ask your friends for their favorites, or use those listed in this book. Post a new quotation on your wall each week. Look at it regularly, contemplate its meaning, and let it inspire you.

The Quilt of Life

Instead of making a quilt from store-bought patches, collect together remnants from old clothes you no longer wear and discarded cushions and fabrics that are past their useful life. Ask your family to contribute too. A quilt sewn from these things will have the added charm of being a jigsaw of personal memories.

Feng Shui at Work

Organize your work station according to the principles of feng shui to encourage a harmonious atmosphere and maximize your efficiency. Declutter your working environment, and put a vase of fresh flowers where all can enjoy their beauty. Surround yourself with positive symbols. Display inspiring quotations, and take the time occasionally to dwell on their special significance for you. Change both the flowers and the quotations before they lose their appeal.

AFFIRMATION

I have work I love that expresses who I am and offers room to grow. My skills and interests open new doors.

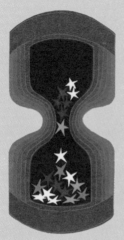

RATION YOUR TIME

All too often, in the face of regular routine tasks, we can find ourselves getting easily distracted from them, or avoiding them altogether. Set yourself mini-deadlines during the day for the completion of potentially open-ended jobs, such as sorting your backlog of emails or doing some of the housework. Such incentives will help you get through the work more quickly, and with a sense of positive achievement.

Stretch at Work

Try this shoulder stretch at work to relieve tension. Sitting on a chair, stretch out your arms and take a few deep breaths. Lifting your right arm over your head, bring your hand, palm down, onto your back. Stretch your left hand behind your back, palm up, and try to hold your right fingertips. Hold the position for a few moments, relax, and repeat on the other side.

A Bird's-Eye View

If ever you feel that your work—in or out of the home—has become a treadmill, step back for a moment and visualize yourself soaring high above the panorama of your life, seeing the whole picture. To revitalize your sense of purpose, look at the positive impact your work has on those around you, and see how it contributes to the wider endeavor.

"Happiness comes when your work and words are of benefit to yourself and others."
The Buddha (c.563–c.483 BC)

AT PLAY

The Spirit of Dolphins

The quality of our lives greatly improves when we take time to play. Schedule play breaks into your daily routine, and whenever you get a chance to lower your guard of logic, seriousness, and maturity, do so—within the limits of civilized behavior, of course. Relaxing like this can help you be more focused and purposeful. Whenever the task at hand needs a injection of new life, let your energies borrow the joyful, energizing spirit of dolphins frolicking playfully in the ocean.

A Playful Retreat

Retreats need not only be for meditation and detox. Why not use your next period of solitude to try to recapture something of the child you once were? Put adult issues on hold. Imagine you are five years old, with a child's curiosity. You may be skilled at crossing the road, but that does not mean that childlike wonder is lost to you. It's playtime, so go and recapture it!

EXPLORE MOVEMENT

True self-expression can involve the body generally, and more particularly the limbs, as well as the brain or the hands. Dancing is a great way to express yourself artistically without pretension—you are not aspiring to produce an artifact, only striving to use time creatively and express something of your feelings, or your sense of yourself and your relationship with fellow dancers.

> *"Mix a little foolishness with your prudence —*
> *it's good to be silly at the right moment."*
> Horace (65–8 BC)

CHAPTER 4

INSPIRING THE FUTURE

Life is constantly evolving. Nevertheless, many of us resist change, preferring the predictability of habit. Our set ways of thinking make us feel safe, secure in the misguided belief that we know more or less what's coming next. But how can we grow, how can we realize our true potential, if we never dare to leave our comfort zone?

This chapter shows you how to take the plunge and prepare for a better future. It will guide you as you face the unknown and set yourself achievable goals to fulfill the unique destiny that is your birthright.

"Life shrinks or expands in proportion to one's courage."
Anaïs Nin (1903–1977)

FACING THE UNKNOWN

✦

Be Open to Change

In life nothing is certain—we forever fall through the emptiness of not knowing. Unable to feel comfortable with such uncertainty, we may close our eyes to the full potential of our lives, clinging to the illusions of safety offered by habit and routine. However, to live fully we must open our eyes and accept our fears of the unknown. We must allow chance to play its part. We must take risks from time to time.

The Future You Deserve

To encourage an abundant future, imagine looking through an open doorway onto a beautiful landscape. The scene is rich with images of all that you hope to experience—perhaps doves symbolizng peace, a pair of swans symbolizing true love. Now imagine stepping through the doorway into the promising future you deserve.

ENDLESS LIGHT

Consider the sun and how it endlessly pours out energy and light onto our world. When you find yourself feeling anxious about the future, imagine the bright rays of the sun penetrating the darkness of the unknown and illuminating your path forward. Just as day follows night, so light will reveal the unknown.

"Once I have determined to move toward enlightenment, even though at times I might become fatigued or distracted, streams of merit pour down from the heavens."
Shantideva (c.700 AD)

Yin Yang

The Chinese yin-yang symbol reflects the opposites that make up the world—light and dark, male and female, positive and negative. The opposing forces are interdependent, each carrying within it the seed of the other. Think of this symbol whenever times get hard. Even in the gloomiest situation, there is always a spark of hope.

"Through meditation upon light and upon radiance, knowledge of the spirit can be reached and peace can be achieved."
Patanjali (c.200 BC)

The Wizard

The wizard symbolizes the wisdom that comes with age.
Imagine yourself gaining power as the years settle on
your head like snow. Visualize snowflakes falling slowly,
adding to your store of insights. Reflect on the vast
knowledge that humankind has accumulated since the
first flake fell to earth. As you age, more of this knowledge can be yours.

The Shining Bridge

The end of one phase in life and the beginning of the next is an artificial turning-point, but one with symbolic significance that can be turned to your advantage. To honor this time, envisage a golden bridge in your mind's eye, connecting the old phase with the new. As you move forward across the bridge, picture yourself taking with you into the future only those qualities and intentions that are wholesome and positive.

Positive Risks

The circus tightrope is a vivid modern symbol of risk-taking. Risks are an integral part of an informed life. We take a risk when we offer love or explore our creative talents and put them on show for others. Leaving the safety of our comfort zone can feel scary, almost as if we are holding our breath in anticipation of reaching the other side of the tightrope. However, when we follow the spirit, the energies of the universe support us.

"It is not because things are difficult that we do not dare; it is because we do not dare that they are difficult."
Seneca (4 BC/1 AD–65 AD)

GOALS

◆

DESIRES AND EXPECTATIONS

Our wishes and expectations are often at odds with each other. To achieve our most cherished goals we need to close the gap. Write two lists: One of your wishes, one of your expectations. Review the wish list. If there's something you feel is worth working for, annotate the item with positive steps you can take. Then modify the expectation accordingly. You now have a program for fulfillment: Put it into action.

Reaching Your Goals

To realize our dreams we have to turn them into goals. Once you have done this, close your eyes and visualize yourself at the bottom of a staircase. How long will it take you to achieve your dream? What is the first step you have to take? What is the second? Imagine the ascent as clearly as you can. Resolve to take the first step today.

The Secret of Long Life

The Chinese character for longevity resembles a labyrinth. Imagine that each worthwhile project you have, whether it is to mend a quarrel or eat more healthily, extends your life in a way that is even more valuable than adding years to your allotted span. Out of a full life comes spiritual peace and a store of memories.

AFFIRMATION

My journey is deep into myself, down a thousand ladders. My horizons expand with every downward step.

The Threefold Path

Think of three things you wish to achieve in the next year. Perhaps you would like to redecorate your home or gain promotion at work. Imagine yourself achieving them in as much detail as possible—see how good that makes you feel. Now formulate a campaign to bring your three goals to fruition by writing down a ten-step strategy for reaching each goal. Start today, and each time you take a step closer to achieving success, give yourself a little reward!

Listen to the Waterfall

Imagine you are walking through a dense forest in search of a waterfall. The best way to locate this wonder of nature is by stopping to listen, then heading toward the sound. Your own steps through the undergrowth prevent you from hearing it. Likewise, you need to step back from your life occasionally, and check that you are still traveling in your chosen direction.

"If you can look into the seeds of time and say which grain will grow, and which will not, speak then to me."
William Shakespeare (1564–1616)

THE RIGHT PATH

When confronted with dilemmas, we frequently have a clear sense of intuition, but often we ignore our hunches and make decisions based on reason—perhaps to find in the end our intuition was right all along, If you feel logic overruling your intuition, close your eyes and imagine the right course of action as a ball of light rising from your stomach and filling your mind with truth. Follow this truth, for it will always lead you along the right path.

Seasons of the Soul

We know that nature's cycles cannot be rushed. Nature has a rhythm of its own. Similarly, our inner lives develop in their own way. Keep this in mind when setting goals. Create a realistic schedule that does not force the pace. In time you will see positive signs, like the first leaves and flowers unfurling in spring.

"Live with a Zen awareness and no more worries about not being perfect."
Seng Jsan (c.520–606 AD)

Thinking Time

Pause to think at different stages of your ambitions. Once you have put into place a strategy to achieve your goals, be patient. Take time to relax and recharge yourself while you sit back and watch your labors bear fruit. This will also give you valuable thinking time in which to plan your next phase and make any necessary adjustments to your current goals.

Reviewing the Grail

Often our goals will change as we journey through life, and so they should: to strive for an inflexible goal can be dangerously extremist. Ask yourself from time to time whether your Grail is still worth the effort. Be prepared to change direction if circumstances so dictate.

The Art of Patience

Many things take time to reach fulfillment—like bulbs, they unfold and flower. Through patience, we can avoid some of the emotions that can spring from impatience—notably, frustration and anger—and also some of the mistakes caused by haste. Make patience a part of your life.

"Do not lose courage in considering your own imperfections, but instantly set about remedying them—every day begin the task anew."
St. Francis de Sales (1567–1622)

DESTINY

✦

YOUR LIFE'S PATH

We all have a unique path to follow. For some it is a central goal to nurture children in body and spirit. Others focus on a fulfilling career, or on some form of creative self-expression, or on a larger contribution to society. To find your life's path, ask yourself what you would most like to offer this world. If you can give a thoughtful answer to this question, you are more than halfway toward knowing your calling.

Signs along the Way

Once you set out with determination on a particular path in life, appropriate signs will often materialize, attracted to your purpose as if by a magnet. If you have this experience, relish it, for it suggests you have chosen wisely.

D\ecision Q\uest

We all reach major turning-points—or even crises—in our lives when a decision is required. The following technique may help to clarify the choice. Picture yourself standing at a crossroads and imagine a pathway for each possibility. Taking each path in turn, project your awareness along the trail. Visualize the sequences of cause and effect to which that route might lead. Note down your findings. The best pathway for you will become clear.

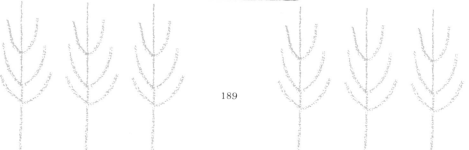

Surf to Your Destiny

Imagine yoursef as a surfer preparing to ride a big wave. You leap onto your board, poised to catch the wave as it surges forward. As the water swells beneath you, you align your board with the direction of the wave. Riding high along the breaker you feel exhilaration as the wind rushes through your hair and the cold spray makes your skin tingle. Now visualize yourself coming safely to rest on the beach. Delight in your sense of achievement.

Shared Experience

Like a shoal of fish swimming as one in the ocean, humankind is bound together by a common destiny. While finding your own path in life, draw strength from the knowledge that everyone around you is also on a journey. You are never completely alone.

"I try to teach my heart to want nothing it can't have."
Alice Walker (b.1944)

LIFE DESIGN

Look at the design of your life. Does every day hold moments of special significance, such as keeping a promise to yourself or to another? Give priority to what fulfills you. Wake up to your real needs, and create a new life design around them. Keep the design flexible, so you can readily adapt it to changing circumstances and interests.

"The quiet, solitary person apprehends the inscrutable—seeking nothing, holding to the middle way, and remaining free from attachments."
I Ching (c.300 BC)

The Mountain

Think of your life's purpose—your highest goal—as a mountain. Most mountain peaks can be scaled if we have the will, the strength, the skill, and the right equipment. However, if we believe that we can achieve such a goal quickly, we may fall victim to our own presumption. We can climb mountains, but only by proceeding one step at a time. Be realistic in your expectations.

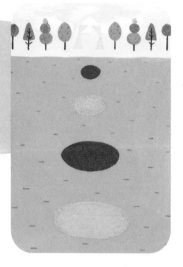

Stepping Stones

No one can expect to make a smooth, steady line of progress toward their goals, like a series of evenly-spaced stepping stones. You should not feel disappointed if, on any one day, you make only half your intended progress, or even no progress at all. But the mere act of thinking about your goals will bring you closer to them. Remember, too, that two steps forward and one back is still a net gain.

Unique Excellence

Allow yourself time to nurture the seeds of your spiritual ambitions. When defining your destiny, beware of the pitfall of drawing upon society's ready-made achievement patterns, such as the pre-packaged models of excellence shown on TV and in the movies and advertising. You will have your own specific destiny, unlike anything anyone has done before. Take pride in your uniqueness—and follow the path even though you may be traveling alone.

Looking Back at the Path

Everything we do or say has effects that ripple outward into the world—however solitary or private our behavior. Try to live life in such a way that whenever you stop and look back at the footprints you've made, you see a path that you are happy to call your own—and one that you feel others might benefit from following.

"Sometimes the most important thing in a whole day is the rest we take between two deep breaths, or the turning inwards in prayer for five short minutes."
Etty Hillesum (1914–1943)

YOUR INNER LANTERN

When we have to make difficult decisions, other people—
even those we love and admire—sometimes question the
paths we choose. However, we should not let this deter us,
because only we can find our own destiny. So venture
bravely: Your inner lantern will light the way.

✦

Fruits of Your Life

Imagine that you are listening in to your family and friends eulogizing at your funeral. What would you hope they would say about your legacy—the good things you did for loved ones, friends, your community, the world? Write down how you would like to be remembered. Now think up ways to turn your legacy into reality, and set yourself a timespan in which to achieve this.

AFFIRMATION
I see that my soul is one among many, all unique
yet alike in one thing: we share the spirit of
the One.

196

Living Library

Visualize a library full of books containing all the world's knowledge. Now imagine that your own contribution to such knowledge—all the unique thoughts that you have communicated to friends and family—arrives in a box of books for the librarian to place on the shelves. Although unpublished, your wisdom can be passed on to others, and some of that wisdom may last down the generations.

Pass on Spiritual Insights

If you discover a spiritual pathway that appears to lead to inner peace, even if you are only part-way along your journey, do not be shy about offering others your insights. Sharing your route to self-realization can only add to the value of your discoveries as they become potential signposts for other people.

A New Generation

Children are closer to their intuitions than many adults. Although their experience of life is limited, their spirit is boundless. Learn from their capacity for play and wonder. In return for their gift of innocence, give them the benefits of your guidance.

"Your children are not truly your children. They are the sons and daughters of life's yearning for itself."
Kahlil Gibran (1883–1931)

RECORD FAMILY MEMORIES

It's never too early to start assembling an archive of family memories—not only photographs but also written accounts, perhaps of conversations you remember. Combine these things with a family tree in a scrapbook or portfolio. A family archive is a special gift to hand down through generations. Making a record is a joint honor you can give to past and future.

A Souvenir of Childhood

True wealth does not reside in possessions, and there is much to be said for regularly decluttering our homes and our lives. However, we should not be in a hurry to discard the most precious reminders of our past, especially of our childhood. Such things are tomorrow's heirlooms—and provide something unique for us to pass on to future generations.

"The words that a father speaks to his children are heard,
as in whispering galleries, by posterity."
Jean Paul Richter (1763–1825)

Earth Watch

We owe it to ourselves and to future generations to make a contribution to the ecological health of our planet. We need to avoid squandering resources such as water, recycle household waste, and buy eco-friendly pesticides and other chemical products. If we are all diligent in doing what we can for the environment, we can keep the world safe for our grandchildren.

CHAPTER 5

INSPIRING THE SPIRIT

There is an eternal life energy, a vital principle that animates all of us. Different spiritual traditions express this belief in different ways. Some speak of the spirit, some of God, some of the Source. Essentially all these traditions agree that the spirit is the fount of all love, of all that we are. If we trust the spirit, we will discover not merely that such trust is justified, but that it is the only thing that makes real sense of our lives and creates true joy.

This chapter suggests many ways to get in touch with your spiritual side—through meditations and visualizations as well as through prayer and creativity.

"Our freedom is but a light that breaks through from another world."
Nikolai Gumilev (1886–1921)

THE DIVINE

The Breath of God

Abbess Hildegard of Bingen, a wise mystic of the Middle Ages, told the story of a king who raised a feather from the ground and commanded it to fly. The feather flew, not because of anything in itself but because the air bore it along. "Thus am I," she said, "a feather on the breath of God." Have faith that you too will become thoroughly attuned to the spirit.

Starry Night

When we look up at the night sky we are seeing not only a myriad twinkling stars but the history of our own universe and a million other universes, whose light has taken eons to reach us. The night sky is a marvelous lesson on the miraculous infinity of time and space.

"Knowledge is limited. Imagination encircles the world."
Albert Einstein (1879–1955)

INNER PEACE

✦

Light on Troubled Waters

We each have an inner light to help us navigate troubled waters. Imagine your light floating just behind your eyes: The more you concentrate on it, the brighter it becomes. Whenever you feel unsure of yourself, reflect for a few moments on your inner lighthouse, and you will never stray far from the right course.

Liberating the Spirit

Sit in a relaxed posture and carry out a bird visualization to help banish care and soothe your spirit. Choose a particular species of bird that is local to your area. Imagine it soaring across a familiar patch of landscape. Feel in your shoulders the effort of taking off—then feel your shoulders relax as you settle into the easy rhythm of flight. See woods and rivers pass below you. Imagine the experience of settling in the treetops. Here you look around in all directions, then become still and watchful as your visualization comes to an end.

AFFIRM THE DOVE

If you adopt the dove as your symbol of inner peace, it will never fail to come to your aid. Consider what the dove symbolizes—love, compassion, truth. Nurture these qualities in yourself by meditating on the dove that resides peacefully within you.

AFFIRMATION
Daily I will visit my oracle: the still voice of peace
that whispers wordlessly in my heart.

The Heart of the Maze

Labyrinths symbolize the journey toward spiritual truth. Visualize yourself walking slowly through a maze, and as you make each turn—now this way, now that—imagine that you are shedding your worldly attachments. When you reach the heart of the maze, you feel purified and renewed. Stay a while before you retrace your steps through the maze and rejoin the world.

"Every step in every proud life is a run from safety to the dark, and the only thing to trust is what we think is true."
Richard Bach (b.1936)

INNER STRENGTH

✦

The Rainbow

In times of difficulty, look to the heavens to lift your spirits. Picture a rainbow and ponder how something so beautiful could emerge from a dark and violent storm. Meditate on each of the rainbow's colors, then let the spectrum dissolve into a beam of pure white light. Reflect on the oneness this signifies, and feel the healing power of spiritual harmony filling you with peace.

Give and Take

When life's demands seem overwhelming and we are giving constantly to others, it is easy to neglect ourselves. Visualize yourself as a pitcher pouring out your love to all around you, then giving yourself an emotional refill. Take a few minutes each day to nurture yourself. The key to true happiness is a balance of give and take.

Into the Canyon

Imagine yourself standing at the rim of a canyon of barren, red rock. As you descend the air dampens and lush greenery envelops you. When you reach the river at the bottom of the canyon, you wade into shallows and immerse yourself in the water. As you do so a sense of power courses through your body—this river is the source of your inner strength, running deeper than you had ever imagined. Repeat this journey whenever you need to call upon your resources of inner strength.

"I have spoken of the light in the soul that is uncreated and uncreatable."
Meister Eckhart (1260–1327)

PINE BRANCHES

Meditate on the pine—Japanese symbol of longevity, fortitude, and silence. Just as we cannot see all the treetops in a pine grove because the background is obscured by the foreground, similarly you cannot predict the exact course your life will take. But if you ensure that, like the trunk of the pine, your inner self is strong and secure, it will support you no matter how far from your roots you grow.

Along the Grain of Nature

We can learn much from the Taoist principle of wu wei: Action through inaction. Essential to wu wei is not to exert pointless effort or to go against nature: Both are thought to lead to the opposite of the desired result. Strength sometimes comes more from doing nothing— and allowing matters to resolve themselves.

Inner Quest

When life's journey seems difficult, use this visualization to give you strength. Imagine you are approaching a walled town on foot. You struggle to penetrate the gates, but you succeed and find yourself in a web of confusing, narrow streets. Undaunted, you persevere, trudging on until finally you find sanctuary in a peaceful, leafy square.

"Just as the path of the birds or the fish is invisible, so is the path of the possessors of wisdom."
Dhammapada (c.3rd century BC)

HARMONY & BALANCE

❖

Tree of Life

In Hebrew texts the Tree of Life is seen as an embodiment of the soul's journey back to the Source. The tree's fruits are the good things given to us by the divine—the harvest of virtues, including love, compassion, peace, and self-awareness. In the vital essence that rises through its trunk and runs through its branches the tree harmonizes all the possibilities open to humankind. In this way it stands as a symbol of the entire universe.

Five-Pointed Star

The pentacle is a symbol of cosmic union. Comprised of two interlocking triangles, it forms a five-pointed star. The triangle pointing upward indicates the masculine, heaven principle; the triangle pointing downward, the feminine, earth principle. Reflecting on the symbolism of the pentacle will help to harmonize the complementary energies of masculine and feminine within your nature.

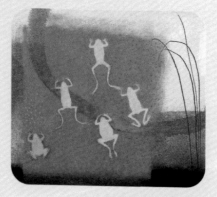

LIVING IN BALANCE

We attain the greatest sense of well-being when we pay equal attention to the physical and the spiritual worlds we live in. Like the frog that effortlessly slips between the elements of land and water, we live in the two realms of body and spirit. Remember to nourish both, to derive the greatest joy and value from life.

AFFIRMATION
I live in the spirit, at ease with body and mind,
with nature in its infinite richness, with others in
spiritual kinship.

The Wishing Well

It is important for all of us, male and female alike, to stay in touch with our nurturing side. Imagine that you are drinking water from a well—a traditionally feminine symbol. The sweet, clear water—the essence of life—refreshes and relaxes you. Now make a wish. In your mind's eye, drop the wish into the well, and give thanks to Mother Earth for her bounty.

PRAYER

◆

Connect through Prayer

Prayer is a way of connecting with the spirit and with others. Imagine your prayer being carried through the air by a flock of birds which take it all around the globe, seeking out similar prayers from other people. Perhaps in such company it will grant you all you wish for.

"God has two dwellings: one in heaven, and the other in a meek and thankful heart."
Izaak Walton (1593–1683)

Widening Circles

Places of worship, of any denomination, can offer a quiet, atmospheric retreat—even in the heart of the city. Find a church, temple, or synagogue near your home or work and use it for meditation, or just for spending a quiet half-hour, refreshing your energies. (If the religion is not your own, ask if you are welcome before taking a seat.) Meditate on any sacred art on display, or on the sunlight that streams in through the windows.

Personal Pilgrimage

Plan a personal pilgrimage to a special place. This could be the oldest place in your neighborhood (such as a historic site or an old elm) or somewhere atmospheric and sacred (like a church or a beautiful spot in nature). Immerse yourself in these surroundings. Open yourself to the place and its positive energy.

"Gratitude is not only the greatest of virtues, but the parent of all others."
Cicero (106–43 BC)

ELEMENTAL GIFTS

The sages of antiquity believed that the four elements—
earth, air, fire, and water—were energy forces that sus-
tained the world. Meditate on the profound power within
each element, and on the enormity of their combined
force. The elements are the materials of life itself. Then
compose a prayer of thanksgiving to the elements for all
that they give us, such as solidity, breath, warmth, suste-
nance. If you prefer a more up-to-date approach, you
could create a similar prayer around the elements of the
Periodic Table—hydrogen, oxygen, carbon, and so on.

CONNECT WITH SPIRIT

✦

Seeds of Promise

Children are full of promise, and we naturally wish to nurture and support them in their endeavors to reach their full potential. However, at any age we retain the ability to develop. Find the promise within you and apply the same kind of care to your own spiritual growth as you would to that of a child—it's never too late to fulfill your potential.

"Every blade has its angel that bends over it and whispers,
'Grow, grow.'"
Talmud (6th century AD)

Divine Image

We know the spirit by names, such as God, the Divine, Beloved, or the Source, but it's hard to give it an actual shape. Spend a moment considering how the spirit looks. In what guise would it appear to you? Now take a sheet of paper and some colored pencils or paints and draw or paint your personal image of the spirit. It can be as figurative or as abstract as you like. Keep your image to help you connect at times when the spirit seems far away.

A Single Drop

Imagine you are a drop of water in the sea. There are billions of drops, and together you form an ocean of waves. If there were no drops, there would be no ocean. In the light of this comparison, meditate on your own spirit. You are one among the many, all unique yet alike in one thing: You share the spirit of the One.

Celebrate the Departed

When someone close has died it is only natural to feel grief and anger at their loss. But take time, too, to celebrate their life, and to give thanks for joyful times together. Share your recollections of the person with friends and relatives and look back on happy memories of the individual when he or she was most alive and fulfilled.

AFFIRMATION
At the center of my being I see a still point of
light—radiant and pure. This is my spirit, the
alpha and omega of my life.

THE LIFE OF THE FLAME

A candle consumes its wick, yet we do not value the flame any less for being exhaustible. Think of life as a positive and miraculous illumination, as you gaze into a candle flame and watch its flickering. However wayward the movement of the flame, there is also something enduring about it—like the divine light at the center of every human being.

The Lotus Blossom

The Hindu tradition sees the lotus as a symbol of spiritual enlightenment, because it rises from mud and darkness to blossom in sunlight. Whenever you feel the need to reconnect with your inner self, visualize a beautiful lotus blossom floating on a pond. Imagine light emanating outward through its petals, to encircle you and fill you with radiant calm, restoring harmony to your life.

Life's Repeating Cycles

Broadly speaking, we all tend to go through similar patterns of experience—from infancy to old age. In one sense we are repeating the actions of our parents and grandparents. Ask yourself what gives spiritual meaning to your life? What is your own special truth? If you are able to discover and live by this truth, the cycle of fundamental experiences—learning, loving, nurturing, working—will be experienced at a higher level.

The Scallop Shell

The scallop shell is a beautiful sculpted gift from the sea. It symbolizes receptivity, the feminine principle, the faculty of intuition. Only by remaining open do we make space for ourselves to receive life's blessings. Receptiveness is a magnet for the profound satisfactions that are available to us. As you meditate, visualize your own spirit opening up like a scallop shell.

Shared Adventure

Share your spiritual quest, and your deepest ideas about spiritual matters, with your partner. Revealing such thoughts can take you to another level of intimacy. You may differ in opinions about the divine, the afterlife, or even morality, but to enjoy companionable dialogue as you travel together on your parallel paths can be one of life's most profound and pleasurable experiences.

"You must trust and believe in people or life becomes impossible."
Anton Chekhov (1860–1904)

A NOBLE CALLING

Integrity is the refusal to break your own rules, which you have based upon your most deeply cherished values. Imagine yourself as the champion of those values, and pride yourself on keeping to your chosen course in life. This is true nobility. It is a full-time occupation—but immeasurably rewarding.

CREATIVITY & SPIRIT

Hidden Worlds

Make a mental list of the many worlds hidden from our view—not only the sea, but caves within the earth, and even the hidden recesses of our bodies. Consider how powerful the imagination must be, to summon these mysteries. The spirit, which may be seen as the grandparent of the imagination, is more powerful still.

"Your playing small doesn't serve you. There is nothing enlightened about shrinking."
Nelson Mandela (b.1918)

Divine Music

Sacred music—whether a classical Indian raga, a Tibetan Buddhist chant, or a Christian gospel song—can give voice to otherwise inexpressible experiences of the spirit. Try playing some gentle sacred music as a prelude to meditation—the finest pieces can feel like a conversation between the individual soul and the eternal divine.

The Poetry of Spirit

"In the beginning was the Word," the Bible tells us. And certain words are deemed to have a magical power in many religious traditions. This is why so many people today are rediscovering the power of poetry. Seek out some of the great poems about the spirit—anything from the medieval Persian poet Rumi to Walt Whitman's "Song of Myself." Poetry like this is a timeless treasure.

Divine Glimpses

The sacred art of the past often has a message of timeless and universal relevance. If you get the chance to see a collection of paintings by a great artist such as Giotto or Titian, give yourself plenty of time to let the images seep into your mind. Such sacred paintings may open your heart to a new experience of spiritual belief.

AFFIRMATION
I see beauty everywhere. I help to create a world
that celebrates beauty in all its manifestations.

THE JOY OF NUMBERS

Take a moment to consider the abstract beauty of numbers. For example, look at the calculations pictured here. Adding a further 1 to the numbers at either side of the multiplication sign (making 1111) gives the new total 1234321, and you can continue adding 1s to extend the series predictably. No wonder Pythagoras believed numbers could unlock the secret of the universe!

SPIRIT IN NATURE

✦

The Call of the Wild

You do not have to be a pantheist (someone who believes that God is present in every natural phenomenon) to find spiritual inspiration in nature. Visit natural landscapes whenever you can—the wilder, the better. Drink in the atmosphere. Rejoice in nature's mysteries and feel connected to the Source.

Earth Magic

All gardeners know the sense of oneness with the Earth that comes from contact with the soil. From time to time, take off your gardening gloves and relish the feelings in your hands—the handles of tools, the plants, and the earth itself. Whatever grows in the soil you have worked will be more fully invested with your nurturing self.

"In all things of nature there is something of the marvelous."
Aristotle (384–322 BC)

Sacred Lights

Meditating on nature brings us into contact with the spirit. Close your eyes and visualize the *Aurora Borealis*, or Northern Lights. These shimmering lights can sometimes be observed in the sky in the northernmost latitudes. As you imagine the delicate veils of light falling across the night sky, feel wonder at the mighty power of the Divine that creates such beauty.

The Summit

In many traditions around the world, mountains have long been regarded as sacred places and are believed to possess powerful energies. A mountain summit is therefore an ideal place to unite with the spirit, because you are at the apex of that energy, profoundly connected with both earth and sky, bringing you a sense of rootedness and transcendence.

"I frequently tramped eight or ten miles through the deepest snow to keep an appointment with a beech tree, or a yellow birch, or an old acquaintance among the pines."
Henry David Thoreau (1817–1862)

BORROW GENEROUSLY

The earth gives us so much and we enjoy eating its harvest. When you take food from the earth, it's good to give something back. Express your gratitude by spending some time cultivating your garden, even if this only consists of a single windowbox. Preparing the soil, sowing seeds, pruning, composting, and caring for new plants are all ways of showing your appreciation for the bounteous gifts of nature.

Eternal Sunshine

Meditate on the daily cycle of the sun's journey across the sky as a symbol of the eternal vitality of the spirit, immune to the world's continual processes of change. Visualize the sun rising, proceeding to its zenith, and then gradually sinking into an incomparable sunset. Appreciate the natural beauty of its trajectory.

"If we have our own why of life, we can bear almost any how."
Friedrich Nietzsche (1844–1900)

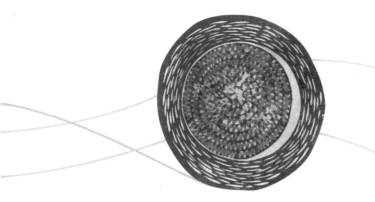

New Moon

Connecting with the cycle of the Moon can help us attune to natural rhythms. Watch the Moon's waxing and waning and notice its effect on your life and emotions—men too can be affected by these phenomena. The new moon, a time for growth, is a good prompt both to plant seeds in your garden and to start new projects in your life.

Animal Beauty

Find a dramatic photograph of a wild animal such as a lion or perhaps an exotic bird—ideally a close-up, showing the eyes. Meditate on the untamable beauty and unfathomable nobility of the creature. Look into its eyes and reconnect with the wonder you experienced in childhood with every fresh encounter. Draw strength from the animal's majestic self-possession.

Sacred Beasts

Our planet belonged to animals before it belonged to us, and in some cultures animals have been revered as gods. Many appear in creation stories. In the Far East, for example, a giant turtle was thought to support the world on its back. By learning about sacred animals we glimpse new ways to see our world and recapture the wonder experienced by our ancestors.

AFFIRMATION

I extend my attention and my compassion to all sentient creatures of the world, and especially to those whose lives depend on me.

ANIMAL KARMA

For anyone who values compassion it is natural to extend concern for fellow humans to fellow creatures. Animals are like people in an important respect—they deserve an acknowledgment of their place in the world. If you show them warmth and kindness, your karma will be enriched. Practical ways to show compassion toward animals range from vegetarianism and humane methods of pest control to adopting unwanted pets.

ACKNOWLEDGMENTS

The Publishers would like to thank Joan Duncan Oliver for her contribution to this book; also, Jane Crediton, Dr. Carl Maraspini, Dr. Benedict Stolling, and Rainer Wagner for help with translations from foreign texts.

The Publishers would like to thank the following illustrators for their contributions to this book: Charlie Baird, Sarah Ball, David Broadbent, Claire Bushe, Trina Dalziel, Nelly Dimitranova, Sandra Dionisi, Hannah Firmin/Sharp Practice, Emma Harding, Katarzyna Klein, Tiffany Lynch, Jacqueline Mair, Peter Malone, Mandy Pritty, Tinou le Joly Senoville and Anne Smith.

Photo Credits

Page 10 Lisa Adams/Photolibrary.com; **64** Fumio Otsuka/Getty Images; **112** Jeanene Scott/Getty Images; **172** Bill Boch/Photolibrary.com; **202** Frans Jansen/Getty Images